What New Orleanians and Friends of New Orleans have to say about "Death, Resurrection, and the Spirit of New Orleans"

"Ken McCarthy is a modern-day Studs Terkel - both are oral historians with a deep respect for Jazz, America's native classical music. In this book, McCarthy illuminates the resurgence of New Orleans through the narratives of the local musicians who experienced it firsthand. An Internet innovator, Ken is the driving force behind Jazz on the Tube, a prominent website esteemed for its daily updates that document the continuum of Jazz history. Accordingly, the site includes audio excerpts from his conversations with these notable musicians, along with an expanding video archive that chronicles contemporary Jazz in New Orleans."

— **Bret Primack, jazzvideoguy.com**

"The author's treatment of "Dirty Dozen" great Roger Lewis was spot on and Brother Chuck Perkins was at the top of his game. Seldom has a book captured the spirit and the soul of our culture in print the way this one has done. The vivid conversation with Ornette Coleman as he recounted his experience in our city while hanging out with the Lastie family was Powerful and speaks volumes for our people and our culture."

— **Al Jackson, Founder and Curator of Treme's Petit Jazz Museum in New Orleans**

"If you're a person who's intrigued by New Orleans and want to take a deep dive into its culture, this book is a great place to start. Ken's passion and love for the birthplace of America's greatest art form shines. Besides jazz representing freedom, it also represents the truth. Ken's new tome is exactly that and then some. My advice? Get this book and get some!"

— **Bobby Sanabria, multiple Grammy nominee, drummer, percussionist, composer, arranger, bandleader, educator**

"Ken McCarthy hosted me for my first visit to New Orleans, and it was a cultural and spiritual revelation. I'll never forget the richness, colour and depth of the culture I met there, or the warmth and friendliness of the people. If you plan to go there, Ken's book makes the best possible introduction; if you can't get there, this book is the next best thing. Enjoy!"

— Grevel Lindop, Poet. Author of "Travels on the Dance Floor", "A Literary Guide to the Lake District", "The Opium-Eater: a Life of Thomas DeQuincy", and several books of poetry.

"I found this small book with its beautiful cover to be a surprisingly deep dive into the deep culture of New Orleans. It's more than a book. It's a guide to a wealth of documentary material concerning the destruction of New Orleans in 2005 by a series of levee failures, and its rescue and renewal thanks to the Crescent City's musicians and culture fans. I enjoyed the stories teased out through dialogue and supported with dozens of videos and audio tracks of the musicians and cultural guardians of New Orleans. It's a book you'll return to again and again."

— Steve O'Keefe, Author of "Set the Page On Fire: Secrets of Successful Writers"

"Ken McCarthy's conversations on New Orleans open into a journey, one man's search through vistas of the music, the culture of the musicians and their chroniclers. Seeking the essence of a world within the city, McCarthy delivers a gladdening read for anyone who loves the music and is curious about the culture-bearers of this fabled town, and their messages that ring out far and wide."

— Jason Berry, Author of "City of a Million Dreams" and "Up from the Cradle of Jazz"

"This unique assemblage of interviews and other archives tells the terrifying but ultimately inspiring story of the near-death and musician-led resurrection of New Orleans following Hurricane Katrina. Ken McCarthy has a deep understanding of the city's life-affirming musical culture, and he pieces together a history of courage and resilience the world still needs to hear."

— **Jack Sullivan, author of "New Orleans Remix", "Hitchcock's Music", "New World Symphonies", and others**

"Ken McCarthy's Death, Resurrection and the Spirit of New Orleans is an absorbing and revelatory collection of conversations with pillars of the New Orleans jazz community, a ringing testimony to that city's bracing resilience in the wake of Hurricane Katrina. McCarthy, founder of Jazz on the Tube, is deeply in love with New Orleans and has a lot to say about it, but he senses correctly that only a polyphony of voices is appropriate to the task at hand: helping us hear and feel the irrepressible spirit of this fascinating city."

— **John Gennari (Professor of English, University of Vermont), Author of "Flavor and Soul", "Blowin' Hot and Cool: Jazz and Its Critics"**

"My uncle was a merchant seaman who shipped out of the Port of New Orleans. He took me there when I was 14 (1945) and the music and the spirit of those who still create it stays in my heart. This book is a treasure chest of true stories that will be shared long after we are all gone. This great book takes us all to school."

— **David Amram, Composer, Conductor, Multi-instrumentalist**

"Whether you are reading Ken McCarthy's text, reading the great interviews, or taking the links to more places and information you are going to love this book. The three ways of approaching the book give a more in-depth idea of New Orleans, its musicians, and its resilience than just one man's opinion. Ken is not afraid to give the reader every opportunity to experience the New Orleans experience in many different ways."

— Mike Vaccaro, musician, educator, producer
MikeVaccaro.com

"Ken McCarthy has a great understanding that New Orleans is the Gateway city when it comes to music in the United States."

— Richard Morse of RAM - The legendary folkloric/roots/ spiritual musical group founded in Haiti in 1990

"An intriguing book about post-Katrina New Orleans by a skilled interviewer filled with little-known information. Shares hard truths, but ultimately celebratory."

— Scott Yanow Author of "Life Through The Eyes Of A Jazz Journalist: My Music Memoirs", and "Jazz on Record: The First Sixty Years"

"This small book was written by a person who rolled up his sleeves and contributed years of effort to helping rebuild the city after the 2005 flood packed its big punch. It's a great entry for people who want a quick read that will help them start on the rewarding road of getting to know New Orleans, its people, and its culture at a deeper level and beyond stereotypes."

— Paul Morrison, jazz pianist

"The first thing I read in Death, Resurrection, and the Spirit of New Orleans is the conversation Ken McCarthy had with Ornette Coleman. The two men agreed that "New Orleans is a real spiritual place," as Ornette said. Admirers of Coleman's music will want to read the whole interview."

— Dave Oliphant, Author of "Texan Jazz: Jazz Mavericks of Texas", and "KD: A Jazz Biography"

"I've lived in the heart of New Orleans for two-thirds of my life, and I do appreciate our culture of music. But there's so much I didn't know until I read this book! Bravo! Also, I can tell you from long years of his unremitting support for Levees.org that New Orleans has never had a better friend or more loyal supporter than Ken McCarthy, the author of this book."

— Sandy Rosenthal, Founder and Director of Levees.org

"Ken has a passion and dedication to the city of New Orleans unlike anyone I know. I moved to New Orleans in 2005 just before Katrina. It changed my life and view of living forever. Ken does not live in New Orleans, but has a unique skill of getting to the heart of a story that he truly cares about. The book is an interesting hybrid, with great links to all sorts of additional information. You can return to it repeatedly for any one degree of separation to anything you need to know about this great place."

— Todd Grove, New Orleans

"A great book. As a former jazz history professor, I really appreciate the "stories of the people"! This book now rests in my bookcase beside my many great jazz books. I highly recommend this book to all enthusiasts."

— Ray James, Associate Professor Emeritus Baker University

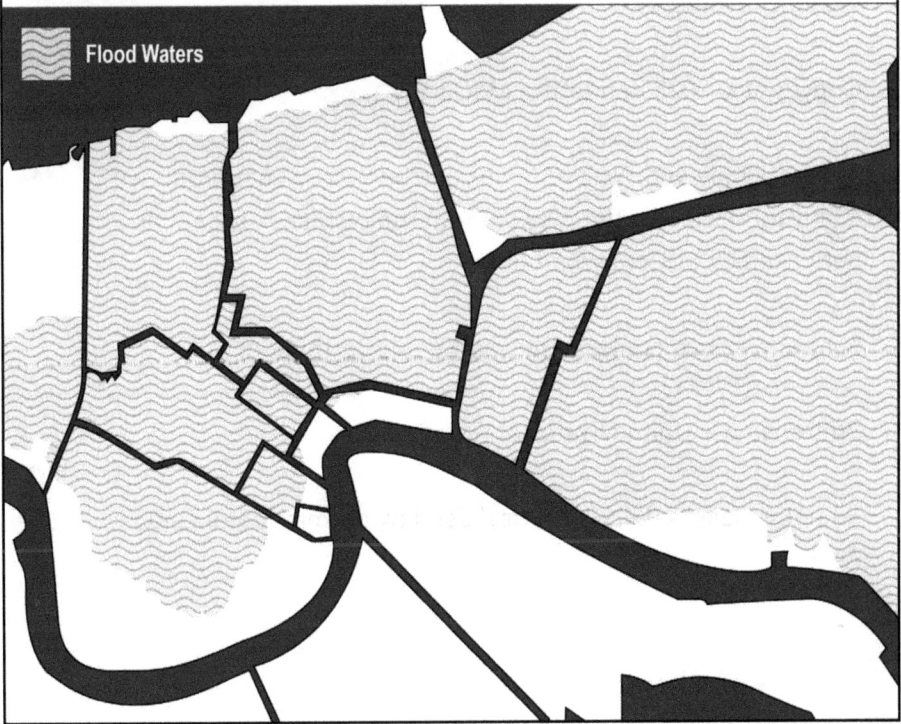
The neighborhoods of New Orleans that flooded in 2005 when the levees failed

Flood Waters

Death, Resurrection, and the Spirit of New Orleans

The Inside Story Of How The Music Brought The City Back From Its Darkest Days

Jazz on the Tube Conversations

Ken McCarthy

Acknowledgments

Thanks to those who
helped make this short book a reality:

To Paul Morrison for keeping the production train of this book on track.

To Taura Hanson for yet *another* great book cover. You spoil me.

To David Yacobucci and Bob Jacobson for kindly helping me catch my innumerable spelling and grammatical errors, helping maintain the illusion that I'm at least semi-literate.

To Bettina Mueller, whose sweet partnership has made more wonderful things possible than I can count.

To Jazz on the Tube supporters. Every year I'm amazed how we continue to grow and move forward. Your support is what makes it possible.

Thanks to the people whose
inspiration and support led me to create this book:

To Steve O'Keefe, an old friend and endless source of inspiration, who gave me a peerless introduction to New Orleans and its music scene.

To Todd Grove, whose extraordinary hospitality and generosity allowed me to find my footing in New Orleans after the flood when congenial housing was hard to come by.

To Julie Carruth, who gave me the opportunity to see New Orleans through the eyes of a multi-generational native.

To Hugie Vigreux, conguero, and filmmaker par excellence.

To Sandy Rosenthal, a warrior who fought harder than any other single person I know for the long-term survival of the ground New Orleans lives on and whose successes need to be included in any serious telling of the city's story.

To Chuck Perkins, the Bard of New Orleans, whose poetry, performed to music, tells the story of New Orleans pre- and post-flood as good as it's ever been told or is ever likely to be told.

To Aurora Nealand, a genuine "musicianeer" (composer, instrumentalist, and bandleader) who does what musicians are supposed to do: channel sonic beauty and bring light to where it's needed. An inspiration since I first heard her at the Spotted Cat in 2006.

And thanks to all the beautiful people I've brushed sleeves with in New Orleans.

This book is for you all!

DEDICATION

"This is for my artists of virtuosity
Who kept the music in the mystery.
For my artistic vanguard
Who came back when times were hard.
Who sometimes came back to nothing
But still came back, underrated and uninsured
Putting their horn where their mouth is."

- Chuck Perkins from Melody Makers ("Lil' Liza Jane")

"No matter where it's played, you gotta hear it starting way behind you. There's the drum beating from Congo Square and there's the song starting in a field just over the trees. The good musicaneer...he's finishing something...that started way back there in the South. It's the remembering song. There's so much to remember."

– Sidney Bechet, *Treat it Gentle*

Table of Contents

Introduction

True story.

I was at the Village Vanguard early so I could get a good seat, namely the red booth against the wall, so close to the stage on the right you're practically sitting with the band. (I enjoy watching music being made as much as listening to it.)

Another fan sat next to me and we started talking. He said he was a drummer. I asked him if he'd ever been to New Orleans.

He said: "Yeah, but it was for a bachelor party and I never got off Bourbon Street."

What?! A drummer who went to New Orleans and didn't spend at least a little time checking out the scene? That's like going to the Vatican and not making it to St. Peter's.

But as the Bible says, "Let he who is without sin cast the first stone," (I was like that drummer once) so I kept my opinion to myself and encouraged him that the next time he went to New Orleans - and he definitely should go again - to roam a bit. It would surely be worth his while.

I grew up in and around New York City and there was a time when I didn't know anything about New Orleans either. Like a lot of New Yorkers, I assumed I lived in the center of the musical universe and that anything that was happening in music was already happening in New York and if it wasn't, it would come by on tour.

My first and only experience of New Orleans, before I went down in early 2006, was in 1990, and it was less than auspicious.

I was driving across the country with my then-girlfriend now-wife Bettina. We were on our way to San Francisco for what turned out to be a long stay, eight years.

Neither of us had been to New Orleans before so we thought we'd check it out.

Even though I was a jazz fan, (radio show host, concert producer, record label grunt), all that I knew about New Orleans then was the French Quarter, Bourbon Street, Dixieland Jazz, Louis Armstrong, and for some weird reason, Ann Rice, who had made the transition from New Orleanian to San Franciscan and back again.

We celebrated New Year's Eve 1990 in Knoxville, TN, and hit the road to New Orleans early in the morning on New Year's Day. We rolled into the city, late and disoriented, and spent the night at what I believe is now called the Canal Street Hotel, now a two-star hotel (a big step up from what it was then), on Canal Street and North Claiborne.

As people who know the city are aware, choosing this of all places to stay was an indication of the depth of our cluelessness. Later when I was living in New Orleans, every time I'd drive past I'd ask myself: "Did we actually voluntarily stay there when we had scores of other options?"

Anyway, we went to bed late January 1, 1990, and woke up January 2, it was a Tuesday, and headed to the French Quarter. Bourbon Street of course. It was overcast and misty, empty to the point of being seemingly abandoned, and stunk of stale beer. Probably what every entertainment district in the world looks like on January 2.

We got some gumbo at a tourist trap and decided, based on this one sample, that the city's reputation for great food was exaggerated. (Cluelessness: Exhibit #2.) I didn't see any signs of music, or more accurately, I didn't see any signs of promising music so, after driving up St. Charles and marveling at the grand homes (they really are a sight), we decided to move on and head west to Texas.

All these unexamined assumptions stuck with me until 2005.

Fast forward to late August 2005. I was in Montreal for a couple of days R & R. I'd heard vaguely that New Orleans was on the path of a hurricane, but didn't know much about it and had the impression it bypassed the city and didn't hit it anywhere near as hard as it hit Mississippi.

Then I saw the news and my jaw dropped. Thousands of people, men, women, children and babies, elderly people, and handicapped people stranded in the city without food, water, or shelter and completely abandoned by the powers that be - and not just for a spell but for days and days on end.

I spent a big part of my vacation sitting on the edge of my bed watching the TV dumbfounded.

The ineptitude and viciousness of government people rarely surprises me, but usually, they make some effort to cover their tracks. In this case, they were letting it all hang out. Day after day no help came.

This in a country with the biggest military in the world, and all the toys that entails. Just two years earlier, justified by a cynical fraud, the U.S. government managed to move 148,000 soldiers with all their uniforms, weapons, ammo, food, and tons of support gear 6,275 miles over the ocean, but somehow it could not deliver emergency food and water to its own citizens on its own home turf in clear weather. Maybe all those UH-60 Black Hawk and CH-47 Chinook cargo helicopters the taxpayers had paid for were in the shop, or maybe they were in Iraq?

Anyway, I was stunned by what I saw and a few months later when my friend Steve O'Keefe invited me to visit him in New Orleans, I jumped at the chance. When I arrived, Steve did the smart thing. Yes, we drove to the Lower Nine and saw the equivalent of a city that had been saturation bombed for weeks (the result of the sudden collapse of the walls of the Industrial Canal, incorrectly designed and improperly built by the U.S. Army Corps of Engineers), but mostly he took me to hear music.

We went from place to place (Steve had a car) and the variety and quality of music on a non-holiday weekday night in a city that was still many years from finding its legs again, amazed me. The street and traffic lights didn't work, the schools were closed and most of the kids were still gone. Tourists were a rare sight and more businesses were closed than open, and those that were open were struggling with countless challenges. But the music was off the hook.

It reminded me of growing up in New York in the '70s where in a single week it was possible to see The Talking Heads at CBGBs, Charlie Palmieri in a free concert in the park, and mind-bending loft jazz performances by people like Lester Bowie, David Murray, Oliver Lake, and others.

The highlight of Steve's tour was a late-night stop at Vaughan's in the Bywater. The neighborhood looked abandoned and we were practically the only people in the small room. The Treme Brass Band was playing. I'd never heard music like this before, "old" tunes played joyously and masterfully, and with absolutely raw power. It was that night I realized that I'd wasted at least half of my musical life. Then and there I decided to make up for the lost time.

Thanks to friends made and projects I got involved in, I was in New Orleans on and off, three months here, five months there, for the next five years.

I learned four things:

1. New Orleans is wildly under-appreciated even by many residents and frequent visitors to the city.

In terms of sheer musical firepower, New Orleans can go head-to-head with entire countries like Cuba and Brazil, its contribution to world music has been that large.

I say "world music" because the New Orleans sound is not just traditional jazz. It played a formative role in the development of gospel, R & B and rock and roll, funk, and the brass band phenomenon that has swept the world in recent years.

2. New Orleans is a paradise for musicians and has more world-class musicians per capita (even if they may not be known beyond the city) than any place I know.

Ever-escalating rents have made it less of an economic paradise for musicians in recent years, but with an abundance of places to play, a culture that includes live music in every phase of life, and a community of musicians who are supportive of each other, New Orleans probably has the best overall musical culture of any city in America.

In addition to the century-plus of past and present marquee performers New Orleans has birthed, the city's music scene made a big imprint on the art of musicians we don't normally associate with the city. People like Lester Young, who grew up chasing the city's parades, Ray Charles who honed his chops at the Dew Drop Inn, and Fort Worth-born Ornette Coleman who said he learned he could play "free" in Frank Lastie's church during an extended stay in the city when he was 19.

The Allman Brothers, pioneers of southern rock, found an enthusiastic audience for their extended jams at The Warehouse, a nightclub in New Orleans. After graduating from Berklee College of Music jazz guitarist Emily Remler polished her chops in the city. Motown never recorded in New Orleans, but when New Orleans drummer Smokey Johnson went to Detroit to record some sides in 1963, Motown founder Berry Gordy and his studio musicians sat up and took notice and you can hear it in the change that took place in their sound afterward.

3. New Orleans is deep.

How deep? I don't know and I'm pretty sure neither I nor anyone else is ever going to get to the bottom of it.

Every time I think I "get" it, I find myself exposed to another dimension. The past lives in New Orleans to a greater degree than most places I've been and interestingly, far from being exotic, New Orleans is one of the most "American" places there is. Parades, live music at social and community events, neighborhoods where people know and say "hi" to each other, all these things used to be staples of American life and they still are in New Orleans.

4. New Orleans food is *really* good. You just have to ask around and find the right places.

* * *

Spending extended time in New Orleans in the years right after the flood was one of the great adventures of my life, made all the better by having found some helpful things to do while I was there.

What I couldn't help but notice during that time was how fundamental the contribution of the city's musicians was to the rebuilding of the city.

John Swenson captured this story beautifully in his book *New Atlantis: Musicians Battle for the Survival of New Orleans*. So did Chuck Perkins in a poem set to the music of *Lil' Liza Jane*.

I hope this story is never forgotten and that's a big part of the reason for this book.

In these pages, you'll meet John and Chuck, along with Roger Lewis, the musician, and Ronald Lewis, the archivist and community leader. They help flesh out some of what makes New Orleans so deep and a city like no other.

By lucky coincidence, in 2006 (still the pre-smartphone era), a company called Pure Digital Technologies started marketing a thing called the Flip

Video camera. It was the size of a pack of cigarettes and had a pretty good camera and surprisingly good sound. Once you filled it up, you could download it to your personal computer, erase the drive with the push of a button, and have another hour of blank canvas to work with.

I took that camera with me everywhere and used it often. When John Swenson and I were talking about his book, it turned out that a surprising number of the events and people that he considered essential to the story of the rebuilding of New Orleans were captured on my camera. I produced some "real" videos too. The video part of this book makes for a good supplement to the text. It's in the appendix called "Videos and Other Resources."

New Orleans was rebuilt by spirit. Thus the title of this book.

The spirit was carried by many people, but first among equals were the musicians of the city.

They were the first back. The first to set up shop. The first to say with their horns and keys and strings and sticks and skins and voices: "This city must come back. This city will come back."

And they did it at a time when a large part of the country had been media-brainwashed into giving up on New Orleans as a hopeless cause. The bulldozers were metaphorically revving up to plow down large parts of the city and put a corporate Disneyland in its place.

With all due respect to Anaheim and Orlando and places like them, I prefer New Orleans.

I hope this book will encourage visitors to get off Bourbon Street and start the process of discovering the city's real riches. Musicians, in particular, if you haven't explored the city's music scene, you are missing one of the great wonders of the age.

For people who already know the city and love it, I'm hoping the stories we tell in this book have parts that will surprise and delight you and that this is a book you can give to interested friends who haven't visited, or visited only superficially, and say: "Here. This is what New Orleans is really all about."

Ken McCarthy
March 9, 2023

JOHN SWENSON AND NEW ATLANTIS

John Swenson (1950-2022)
in conversation with Ken McCarthy
Recorded in 2011

Ken McCarthy: Anybody who's been a regular listener, viewer, or follower of Jazz on the Tube knows that we love New Orleans. Every chance we get we want to remind people what a great place it is, and how important it is to visit, whether you've been there before or not.

Contrary to some people's strange, misguided notions, New Orleans is not still underwater. There are actually people who believe this. No, it's on dry land, and the music is better than ever. In fact, my friend Ned Sublette thinks the music scene in New Orleans right now is as hot as the music scene was in New York City in the 1970s, which was very hot indeed. And, today we're going to talk about *New Atlantis: Musicians Battle For The Survival of New Orleans* by John Swenson.

I want to start this off by saying: get the book. Get one for yourself. And, if you've got a friend who loves music, who loves culture, who loves travel, who loves history, get it for them as a present. Get it for your local library. Nothing will put a bigger smile on your librarian's face than to see a really good book come in the door. And this is a great one.

This book chronicles one of the most amazing stories in music history intertwined with the history of humankind's experiment with urban living. It is a story about the salvation and rebuilding of a city that was almost entirely wiped off the map by a federal government-made disaster. I'm not talking about a weather disaster by the way. I'm talking about the U.S. Army Corps of Engineers engineering disaster which caused massive levee failures that destroyed countless lives and property.

The heroes of this story are the people who are near and dear to each of us, the musicians who everywhere make the world a better place but, especially and largely, the jazz musicians.

Make no mistake about it. It was the musicians of New Orleans who came back and endured unbelievable and often devastating hardships to relight the flame of New Orleans and got that city back on its feet.

Of course, a lot of people contributed to the city's re-birth, but the musicians' contribution was essential. And, now, John and I are going to dive deep into the details of this remarkable comeback.

So, let's welcome our distinguished guest, John Swenson.

John Swenson: Ken, thank you very much for the wonderful endorsement of the book. And by extension, the great comments you made about all of these magnificent human beings who helped bring New Orleans back, through the force of their culture.

Ken McCarthy: It's one of the great stories of jazz history. We're all familiar with the jazz story beginning with ragtime, going through the Swing Era, the Bop Era, the Hard Bop Era, the Free Jazz Era, and that whole beautiful history. I believe this story has got to be considered one of the most important chapters in the history of jazz. The music, against all odds, helped rebuild a city that many thought was finished.

I want to give the title again, for everybody who's taking notes: *New Atlantis*, by John Swenson. And first, let's give some praise to the publisher.

Now, tell us about the process of getting a publisher to recognize the value of the story, and who finally stood up and did it.

John Swenson: I worked on the proposal for a year. I had been covering New Orleans music since well before the flood. And when I returned to the city, a couple of weeks after the flood, I became obsessed with interviewing the musicians. They all had such harrowing tales about what they went through. And as more musicians returned to the city, the stories just kept building up and building up.

I realized a couple of things. It wasn't just another music story. And the story of "what happened to my house in Katrina" had become a cliché. The fact is these musicians were literally involved in rebuilding the city. Literally involved. Gutting houses, helping to build new houses and opening businesses. Not to mention playing. Playing often for no money. Playing without a place to live. And it occurred to me that these stories were too big and too interconnected to fit into magazine articles. After a while, I realized I had to fashion something larger.

So, I conceived of this book idea. There are so many books about Katrina and several outstanding books about the people of New Orleans before, during, and afterward. Two that come to mind immediately are *Zeitoun* and *Nine Lives*. But this was a different book. This was about the musicians driving the recovery, and it was a difficult concept to sell.

My agent, Sarah Lazin (who's also Ned's agent; you mentioned Ned Sublette earlier), sent the book around to a lot of different people, a lot of different publishers. And we kept getting that "Katrina fatigue" response. But the book isn't about Katrina. It's about what's happened since.

Ken McCarthy: That's like saying, "We've got Mozart fatigue. We've got ancient Rome fatigue." This is a story for the ages. This is not some little news blip.

John Swenson: I understand what you're saying, but that's what we were getting back. I was also getting back responses from editors that were just looking at it as another music book. One response that really sticks in my mind is the guy who said, "Why isn't there a chapter on Sissy Bounce?" (a New Orleans music genre). Now, if you read the book, you'll know that Sissy Bounce is actually included because it was important. But the book is not different chapters on the styles of music in New Orleans. It's a story about musicians.

Amazingly, a lot of editors just couldn't see what was actually in the proposal. And believe me, I worked hard on the proposal. A proposal lays out what's supposed to be in the book. Fortunately, Oxford University Press, a great and prestigious publishing house, signed it and released it here in the United States, as well as in England, and in Canada. The thing about Oxford that I'm very gratified about is their commitment to keeping things in print. So, I'm happy to think that when I'm not around anymore to relate the story to people, the book will be able to inform future generations about what actually happened during this period of time.

Ken McCarthy: There were no birds. There were no animals. There were no children. The city was deserted. It was occupied by the National Guard. The only people who were allowed to return were people who had essential jobs, and a few other people snuck back in.

And if anybody thinks that because it's published by Oxford University Press that it's a dense, hard-to-read tome, it's not. This is beautiful writing, very clear, and very accessible. It's great that a serious publisher is putting its weight behind it. So, thank you Oxford University Press for recognizing the value of American culture. I'm glad somebody in the publishing world does.

Let's remember something about the weeks after. We use "Katrina" as a shorthand, but because I'm involved with Levees.org, and because I believe this is important, I want to let everybody know that the storm was nothing. The storm ripped a few shingles off a few roofs. It was the levee failures – over 50 different levees failed after the storm as the result of bad engineering. This was a man-made, government-made, corrupt businessmen-made disaster, completely unnecessary. It did not have to happen. This point needs to be said and must not be overlooked.

Let's remember what those original weeks were like after the flood. I remember the dead silence, which was so strange. And some of the very first sounds in the city were the sounds of music.

John Swenson: That's right. Musicians played even before the electricity came back on. Then as soon as the electricity came back on, people plugged in and began playing. Coco Robicheaux tells a wonderful story about sitting in his car and seeing the electricity come back on. He ran into Molly's at the Market and he plugged in and started playing. He played for like six hours, and everybody was dancing on the bar. There was a curfew back then, but the National Guard looked the other way in certain instances.

Ken McCarthy: It's interesting you mention the curfew in bars because bars turned out to be very important social gathering places. They allowed for the transfer of news, a place to find old friends and, most important, they were places to let off steam and deal with things. They turned out to be very important social institutions.

John Swenson: The landline at Johnny White's on Bourbon Street (Johnny White's sports bar - there are three different Johnny White's) never went out. So even when you couldn't get through to the city you could call up Johnny White's and the bartender would answer. I hooked some Irish radio broadcasters up with them. It was pretty amusing actually.

Ken McCarthy: One story stands out for me, and there are so many, but one individual who really stands out is the irrepressible Glen David Andrews.

John Swenson: Oh my God.

Ken McCarthy: A member of the Andrews clan, who I believe is related to the Lastie family, another great New Orleans family.

John Swenson: Right. I'd have to go back and look at my notes to trace all of the family roots there. But they were all connected in Treme. Dr. John remembers going over there and hanging out. And he saw Trombone Shorty when he was a little kid playing the tuba when he couldn't even lift it up, just laying down on the floor sideways. But, go back to Glen David for a second. His grandfather was Jesse Hill, the man who wrote "Ooh Poo Pah Doo" and was also in Dr. John's first band when he took the Dr. John name after working as Mac Rebennack for so long.

Glen David Andrews, to me, is the star of the book. His story about being there before the hurricane hit, surviving, and thinking, wrongly it turned out, that he dodged a bullet, like everybody who was there did after the storm passed. Then dealing with the inundation, which affected his grandma's house where he was staying. He fled to the projects and was holed up there. They finally had to get out of town because of the evacuation. And his story of coming back and playing in the square where Tuba Fats had taught him as a young person. Also, his struggles. He had an addiction demon that he struggled with, and he battled it. He had ups and downs. He was very depressed. And he went into rehab at one point. There was this constant evolution where he would make two steps forward and take a couple of steps back and then keep going.

I kept running into him over the years and talking to him. He's such a great conversationalist, and I often had a tape recorder with me. So, just seeing him talk about his life over the course of these couple of years, and then, of course, having this tremendous breakthrough - which you actually have documented on your site with the Heaven's Gate video that you underwrote for Glen. And now his presence in *Treme*, the HBO series. Glen's story is really a wonderful illustration of the transformation that the musicians were able to go through.

Ken McCarthy: There's an important part of the story. It's a sad part of the story, but it's something that has to be part of the chronicle. There were many losses related directly to the levee failures, but there were also a lot of wonderful young people - community leaders, artists, musicians, and educators - who were murdered after the levee failures. I think it was Dinerral Shavers who was the first to suffer that fate. Do you want to talk a little about Dinerral's story?

John Swenson: He was leading a group of young musicians - I should back up for a second. One of the things that was missing after the flood was the marching bands, which people see most prominently at Mardi Gras. There were far fewer young people. The absence of young people in the immediate aftermath of the flood was staggering, and it took a very long time for these marching bands to reassemble. In fact, this was a problem that had been occurring before the flood. And it's a political problem, caused by the deprivation, or the cessation, of funds for music education in the school system in New Orleans.

I don't know what genius came up with the idea, but in a city that relies as much on culture and music history as New Orleans does, the idea of taking the funds away for the marching bands and instruments for young people, whose alternative is to join street gangs, was really stupid. And it's an ongoing problem. The current governor, Bobby Jindal, is against all forms of education it seems. And he's piling on this problem. And, so this is one of the many things that the musicians did to overcome the lack of leadership from all areas of government.

Ken McCarthy: I'd like to make one related point. These marching bands have had really high levels of musicianship. And they are basically the farm team for the whole New Orleans musical community. In other words, the path of development is, as a little kid you follow along with the band and march along and feel proud just to walk next to the musicians. Of course, that puts the idea in your head, "Wouldn't it be great to be one of the guys playing?" Then the next step is when you're in school, you get your instrument, you become part of the band, and you get trained on your instrument. The next part of the evolution is you and some friends get together and create your own brass band, and stake out a street corner to play on. If you're good, you survive, and people start asking you to come and play at parties, and eventually some indoor club gigs. So, these marching bands are really important.

I want to point something else out. And I don't think this is a really well-known fact about jazz history. We always hear about the great jazz greats, and, of course, one of the greatest of the greats was Lester Young. For some bizarre reason, not many people realize Lester Young got a big chunk of his early musical education on the streets of New Orleans. If you find some biographical material of him you will see that as a kid, young Lester Young ran along with these bands, the street bands, not the school marching bands, but the funeral bands and the parade bands. And that was one of his introductions to the world of music. So, this street scene, this parade scene, this marching band scene, it's not your marching bands back home, as important as those are.

John Swenson: It's true. It's very difficult to find a New Orleans-raised jazz musician who didn't have a connection to the marching bands as a child. So, some of the musicians took it upon themselves to raise money to get instruments for these kids and to teach them how to play in brass bands and in marching bands. Dinerral Shavers had a marching band pretty much ready to perform in their first Mardi Gras when he was killed at the end of 2006. It was a great tragedy, and it really rocked the city's music community. It was one of eight murders that took place - I believe it was eight - in the space of a week. And a few days later, the filmmaker Helen Hill was also murdered.

They both had ties to the Sound Café. The people at the Sound Café organized a march on New Orleans City Hall. They organized the group called Silence Is Violence. Glen David Andrews had also been involved in a teaching program at Sound Cafe. He was one of the Silence Is Violence spokespersons as was Helen. They both played a role in organizing the march on City Hall, which brought a lot of attention to this problem. (Editor's Note: Helen was murdered one week before the City Hall rally, which she had helped organize.)

While it couldn't solve the problem immediately, it showed that the citizens of New Orleans were not going to stand back and do nothing while the mayor and police commissioner refused to pursue these cases. This drama was played out very effectively in the second season of the HBO series *Treme*, which details a lot of what we're talking about, and particularly the lack of police homicide detectives to bring any of the murder cases to trial.

Ken McCarthy: We have video of the memorial

parade for Helen Hill. We also have some very rough video - I handed the camera to a friend of mine that really wasn't a camera person - of what turned out to be one of the last, if not the last, performances of Dinerral Shavers. This was at the Big Nine Social & Pleasure Club, their big parade. It was their first big parade after coming back at the end of '06. It was a massive parade with thousands of people in it. The Hot Eight Band, which was the band Dinerral played drums for, was one of the bands in the second line. And, of course, we also have a video of Glen David Andrews' remarks at that very Silence Is Violence gathering that took place outside of City Hall.

As if all the murders weren't bad enough the city had lost just about everything - all its clubs, so many houses, hospitals, stores, traffic lights, electrical lights, sewage pipes, water pipes. The pipes had the weight of 10 to 15 feet of water or more sitting in some neighborhoods for a month. This compacted the soil which, in turn, compressed and broke the pipes. The scale of the rebuilding of New Orleans is easily one of the most heroic things that ever took place in America, a largely untold story.

That's why we're on this interview right now. And, we're talking specifically about musicians, and other artists. People like Helen Hill and Baty Landis who ran the Sound Cafe and founded Silence Is Violence. It was all kinds of artists. And, that's one of the beautiful things about New Orleans. There's a lot of communication among all artists.

I don't want to take anything away from New York. I grew up in New York, and I was exposed to the music in New York, and it's where I got my education and everything, but New York tends to be a place where people are very focused on their careers, and their bands. And, the clubs are a little antiseptic with white tablecloths and big cover charges. The music sets are strictly governed by the clock. That's New York. New York has got to be that way. It's that kind of a city.

New Orleans is another world, a lot of interaction between the different musicians. It's not unusual for a musician to just wander in off the street and see a buddy playing and shout out, and then receive an invitation, "Hey, why don't you come up here and join us?" That kind of thing. A lot of collaborations between musical artists and artists in other genres. It's a very creative, very human place.

We started out by talking about the essential role that musicians played in being among the very first, if not the first, to come back and bring the city back to life. Then we talked about some of the really hard knocks the city took after the flood - as if the flood itself wasn't enough. And how the musicians demonstrated their resilience in the face of all that. Where do you want to go now? There are so many different things we can talk about. The book is so rich and full of stories and personalities. I learned a lot of things from it that I didn't know about the rebuilding.

John Swenson: I'd like to put a little overview on it. New Orleans, in its more than 250 years of existence, has been wiped out numerous times by floods and fires. Several times the city burned to the ground and had to be rebuilt. It was depopulated by yellow fever. It has overcome many obstacles. And it seems that each time a different economic engine has driven the city's recovery. Unfortunately, one of those was slavery. But, also the oil industry, the shipping industry, and the sugar industry, each at different times, were the economic engines.

But this time, I believe that culture is the economic engine that has driven the recovery. Mitch Landrieu, who is last year's newly elected mayor, is a great champion of Louisiana culture. He was the lieutenant governor before he was mayor, and culture was his big angle. So, he's really gone out of his way to try to help the musicians realize their goals.

In the immediate aftermath of the flood, the city officials got together and came up with a plan that was going to include a vast green zone of country clubs and golf courses, museums, casinos, and a kind of Disneyland-style tourist destination for rich people. And, there was a great outcry against this. The thing that in the end did most to stop it was the recession. Otherwise, they were really on the fast track to making it happen. As it was, we've seen the destruction of a huge section of Central City for the new medical center, one of the elements of the plan. At the same time, Charity Hospital, which so many depended on and could have been reopened, was not allowed to reopen. At any rate, the point is that the musicians came back and restored the culture. They brought New Orleans back to a place where music is a central part of everyday life.

We were talking about the difference between New York and New Orleans. In New York and most places, when you talk about culture and music, people pay money to go and sit in a chair and watch a performance. Music is a part of everyday life in New Orleans. So, it's a very different set of circumstances. The music is more in the streets there. It's as much in the streets as it is in the clubs. And I don't know if you could say "for free" because there are all different ways to talk about that, but it accompanies birth, and it accompanies death, and it accompanies everything in between. That is the function that music serves there.

The musicians were forced to leave the city like everyone else. And they were often offered very good terms to reside in places like Portland, Oregon; Austin, Texas; and Brooklyn, New York. But when they got there and started playing, they realized their music didn't have the same context in the community that it enjoyed in New Orleans. The music didn't have the meaning that it has in New Orleans. So, they had to go back to New Orleans, to re-establish their culture, in order to give themselves a context to allow their music to be as spiritually advanced as it is there. It's not entertainment.

A lot of people before the flood thought of the music just as entertainment. Songs like "Do You Know What It Means to Miss New Orleans?" and

"St. James Infirmary" were considered "old" songs. Well, when these musicians came back - when James Andrews came back immediately after the storm (that's Trombone Shorty's older brother, and Glenn David Andrews' cousin) his performance of those songs, which had been entertaining before, brought real new meaning to them. And you could see they had new meaning for him, and for all of the musicians who played them. The point of this book is that these musicians re-established the unique culture of New Orleans through their music.

If you look at another large point, the United States is changing in character, becoming less of a manufacturing base and more of a place where software is produced and ideas are created and intellectual properties are created. This is what is driving the recovery of New Orleans now in terms of culture - the intellectual property of the musicians. And, I think it's a kind of canary in the coal mine for the entire country.

Ken McCarthy: As for music culture in general, what goes on in New Orleans today is the way things used to be everywhere in the country. The school band used to be a highlight, and live music used to accompany everything everywhere. I don't know if you're aware, but way back, there were second lines in Albany, New York, and Philadelphia. So New Orleans, in many ways, is like the last holdout, the last stronghold for America's music culture.

I believe there are two kinds of people in the jazz world; those who've been to New Orleans, and those who haven't. And, I've been on both sides of that. When I was a young guy living in New York, I didn't get out of New York, literally, for years. I never left the island. Brooklyn was a long trip. I thought New Orleans was some ancient history place that had nothing to do with anything. But, when I got down there, I was chagrined at just how profoundly ignorant I was. Not only was New Orleans not an ancient backwater, but New Orleans is in many ways the eternal flame of America's music culture. Just count the things that have come out of New Orleans...

Most people are vaguely familiar with the idea that jazz got its start in New Orleans. And, the case can be made that so did rhythm and blues, and even funk. And to some degree, even the sound of Motown was influenced through the lineage of New Orleans by Smokey Johnson, a New Orleans drummer who visited Detroit in Motown's early days and showed people in Detroit what drumming could be.

When the Beatles came to America, they wanted to meet Elvis Presley, but the guy I think they were really awed by was Fats Domino. There's a picture of the five of them together that tells the story. And, of course, Louis Armstrong is a New Orleans native. Lester Young was born in Mississippi and lived all over the country, but he spent his seedling years right in the heart of New Orleans. You can hear it in his sound, I think, and in his approach to life, and his approach to music. And on and on it goes.

So not only is New Orleans important to the history of this music but it also maintains the spirit of the music. And so, besides encouraging people to get a copy of *New Atlantis*, I encourage everyone to visit and experience New Orleans, especially if you love jazz music.

I'm going to tell you right now, do not go between May and November unless you are really tough because I've seen grown men, multi-generation descendants of cane-cutters, who still weep when August comes around because the weather is just so brutal. Don't think that you've experienced hot weather until you've experienced New Orleans in the summer. You don't know what hot is. John, am I lying?

John Swenson: I have to take exception on one issue. I think everybody should visit Satchmo Summerfest at one point in their lives because it's so wonderful. The annual celebration of Louis Armstrong's birth date is the first weekend of August. Tough it out for a couple of days, because the music is so alive. The earliest moments of jazz still live there.

I might also point out that if you listen to Jelly Roll Morton, you'll hear the roots of everything that's happened since. You'll hear Professor Longhair, and Dr. John... New Orleans is a place that is not cut off from the past, and it's certainly part of the future as well. It's a continuum. The music is an ongoing phenomenon there. And I would like to endorse the Satchmo Summerfest, certainly.

Ken McCarthy: Fair enough. But let's warn people, be prepared to be hotter than you've ever been in your life.

John Swenson: Yes, I would recommend against being out in the hot sun between, let's say noon and 4 pm. Stay out of the sun.

Ken McCarthy: I had a friend who grew up in Brazil, and when she went to New Orleans in June, she could not believe how hot it was. But if you're tough, I think it's certainly worth it to go to the Satchmo Festival. Do that. But if you want to be comfortable, December through April is just lovely weather. Forget California. New Orleans around March or late February when the magnolia trees blossom, you can't get much better weather than that.

Talking about tradition, and talking about Jelly Roll Morton, he talks about the Mardi Gras Indians. And this is a tradition that, if you're in New Orleans, you can't help but see influences of them everywhere, but if you've never been to New Orleans, you may have never directly experienced it, or not even know what the heck it is. Can we talk a little about the Mardi Gras Indians and how important they are to the whole New Orleans scene?

John Swenson: When Africans were brought to the United States as slaves in the early days of the colonies, they interacted with the Native Americans who were around, and they shared a lot of cultural similarities. They were natural allies, who shared, if you will, a common enemy in the colonists who had come to take away what the Native Americans had and had taken away what the now African Americans had enjoyed in their homelands, that is to say, their freedom.

So, there was a strong cultural interaction from the very first days of their meetings, between African Americans and Native Americans. And that, I believe, was the beginning of the creolization process.

The colonial authorities who controlled the official story were very afraid of the potential of the slaves and Indians banding together to revolt. So, they suppressed this connection. But it's a long-standing connection. It's a blood connection. And it's a blood connection that's been hidden.

One of the other main characters in *New Atlantis* is Cyril Neville. One of the stories that it traces is his understanding of his heritage as not just an African American but as a Native American. He found out through his uncle, George Landry, that there was Indian blood in the Neville family. He researched it and made personal connections with various Indian nations, and brought some Native Americans on stage with the Neville Brothers at Jazz Fest. In turn, the Chahta tribe named him their ambassador to the outside world. The Mardi Gras Indians are a reflection of that. They're also called, in the Black neighborhoods, the "Black Indians." There was a French name for black Indians, I don't know all of the details of that, but there have been some really good studies on it.

Ken McCarthy: A fair amount of the history and the culture of it is occult in the sense of its being secret and hidden. Part of it, as you pointed out, is that the powers that be don't want to give credit to these cultural forces. On the other hand, a lot of the traditions of the Mardi Gras Indians are for the Mardi Gras Indian tribe members only. These include parts of the history, the language, and some of the meanings behind the chants. As an outsider, you can't just walk up and "Hey, what are you guys doing?" It's for tribal members. I believe it was a survival mechanism, a survival training. Part of the Mardis Gras Indian culture dealt with the tremendous strains and stresses of living...

John Swenson: It's absolutely true. New Orleans was essentially an apartheid city right up until 1965. As Cyril Neville points out, as a young Black person you had to be able to read so that, as he quotes his aunt saying "so you didn't accidentally stumble onto death" by drinking from the wrong water fountain or going into the wrong restaurant.

Ken McCarthy: There's another, almost ancient connection, which is that during the French period, the Code Noir, which was their rules regulating slavery, permitted Sunday mornings off, and both Africans and Native Americans would congregate in a place that's now called "Congo Square." To understand how profound this is, because a lot of people don't know this history, in British North America, it was illegal to play the drums, under the penalty of death.

John Swenson: Yeah.

Ken McCarthy: That's how frightened the Anglo-American slave enterprise was of the power of this culture, of music in general, and of drums in particular. Of course, in Cuba and Brazil, it was different because it wasn't the Anglo-Americans running things. But the only place in North America where the music was allowed any meaningful breathing room was in New Orleans, specifically in Congo Square, which also happened to be a former sacred spot for the Native Americans.

There almost certainly was personal interaction between Africans and Native Americans there. Africans from all kinds of backgrounds and tribes. People who might not otherwise have ever met each other in Africa were thrown together in New Orleans. It may well be that some of our most important rhythms in American music can be traced back to Mardi Gras Indian rhythms, in which case we're really talking about African and/or Native American rhythms, in a kind of fusion. So, this is pretty deep stuff.

Here's another point of history that every lover of music should know. If you go to Congo Square, just cross the street and walk down, I think, two blocks, you're at the recording studio where basically rhythm and blues, rock and roll was born. It was run by a Sicilian-American, Cosimo Matassa.

Here's another little-known fact. Around the turn of the last century, the French Quarter was about 90% Sicilian. Because they were treated pretty badly,

Cosimo had great sympathy for Blacks and Black musicians as did many Sicilians. And, as far as I know, he was the first man to record black musicians in a formal recording studio in New Orleans. That didn't happen till the '50s. If you ever wondered, why are all these Louis Armstrong sides coming out of Chicago? It's because if you were a Black musician in New Orleans, you were not welcome in a recording studio in the city. It took until the '50s, and it took this one man, to break that. That's a side story, an important one. But the point I want to make about Congo Square and his recording studio, is that if you have a good arm, you could practically throw a rock from Congo Square and hit that recording studio.

John Swenson: Right at Rampart and Dumaine.

Ken McCarthy: Rampart and Dumaine is referenced in a lot of New Orleans music. So, there is something magical about New Orleans and what goes on there, and what goes on to this present day.

And as John documents in his book, *New Atlantis*, when you look at the incredible heroic efforts these musicians made - they lost everything! They lost their homes, all their possessions, often their musical instruments, their cars, their neighborhoods, their communities, their money such as they had. They lost everything and were pushed out of town by this disaster. And they were the pioneers who came back with really no help, and not much support, except from fellow artists and fans. And they re-invigorated the city. And wow, the city's rockin' now. You go down there now and unless you get out a bit and really drive around, you'd never even know that this disaster happened in the main areas.

Let's tell people where they should go. Bourbon Street is worth about five seconds; where you really want to go is Frenchmen Street.

John Swenson: Right. The new music capital. You go from Esplanade and Decatur right around where Checkpoint Charlie's is; you walk right down Frenchmen Street and you're going to pass a dozen clubs where the music just spills out onto the streets. And it's all kinds of music, from the very beginnings of jazz to the very latest hip-hop/brass band fusion, or the nouveau swing that Donald Harrison plays now. The whole history of jazz is on display. And there are a lot of young people there as well who are representing the newer forms of music that exist in the pop landscape.

A lot of young people have moved to New Orleans because it's an affordable place to live. And it's a place to sort of rough it and have an adventure. It's a good place to be young right now; but not a good place to be old, because the healthcare system is bad. And it's a very poor city. But if you can rough it, and like adventure, it's a great place to be right now.

Ken McCarthy: And if you love music, when you get yourself to Frenchmen Street, because I hope everybody listening gets there, you'll meet people. It's a very friendly scene. You will make friends much faster than you can even imagine and people will fill you in on the other spots because there are clubs scattered all around the city. Some of them are in odd places. You just have to know where they are. And you'll figure that out once you get to Frenchmen.

John Swenson: Every other doorway is either a club or a restaurant. Praline Connection is there and The Deli for food, but everything else is a club. There have got to be a dozen clubs, at least, right along the two-block section of Frenchmen Street. I would also like to point out that all of this that we're talking about has been very beautifully portrayed on the HBO series *Treme*. We've had two years of it, and we're going to get at least one more year. And I would like to say that if anybody is a fan of the series, and they are wondering what we're going to see next season, if they pick up a copy of *New Atlantis: Musicians Battle For The Survival Of New Orleans*, they may get some hints about what will be in the next series.

Ken McCarthy: Great! We could easily talk about New Orleans and its history and what it continues to contribute and what it's been through, and how it's evolving, for the next month. But we have to cut it at some point. So, this might be a good place.

We've been talking with John Swenson, author of *New Atlantis: Musicians Battle For The Survival Of New Orleans*. A great book. All praise to Oxford University Press for having the wisdom to put this book out there.

If you love jazz, if you love the music, if you love New Orleans, this is the book. Support this book. Buy it. You might have friends who would like it; it makes a great present. And, don't forget your library. I'm sure, with all the budget cuts they're facing, they would be delighted to receive a book of this caliber for their collection. You never know what happens when you give a book to a library, how many lives will be touched by it.

John, thank you for taking the time to tell us a little bit of the story. I know that the full story is vast and fascinating. And, I am so grateful to you for making sure this story did not get lost.

John Swenson: Thanks very much for your work, Ken. It's been very illuminating.

Ken McCarthy: Great. And maybe we'll run into each other in New Orleans or maybe in New York.

This is Ken McCarthy and John Swenson, saying goodbye, on behalf of Jazz on the Tube. Get yourself a copy of *New Atlantis*.

Watch the videos mentioned in this interview at:
www.JazzOnTheTube.com/NOLA

(1) *The Making of Glen David Andrews' "Walking Through Heaven's Gate."* Directed and edited by Lily Keber. Funded by Ken McCarthy.

(2) *Helen Hill Funeral.* Filmed by Ken McCarthy.

(3) *Dinneral Shavers in the Big Nine parade.* Filmed by Julie Carruth. (2006)

(4) *Glen David Andrews at the "Silence Is Violence rally" at City Hall, New Orleans.* (2007)

(5) *Smokey Johnson and Bob French talk about New Orleans drummers. At the Ponderosa Stomp.* (2008)

See Appendix for more details.

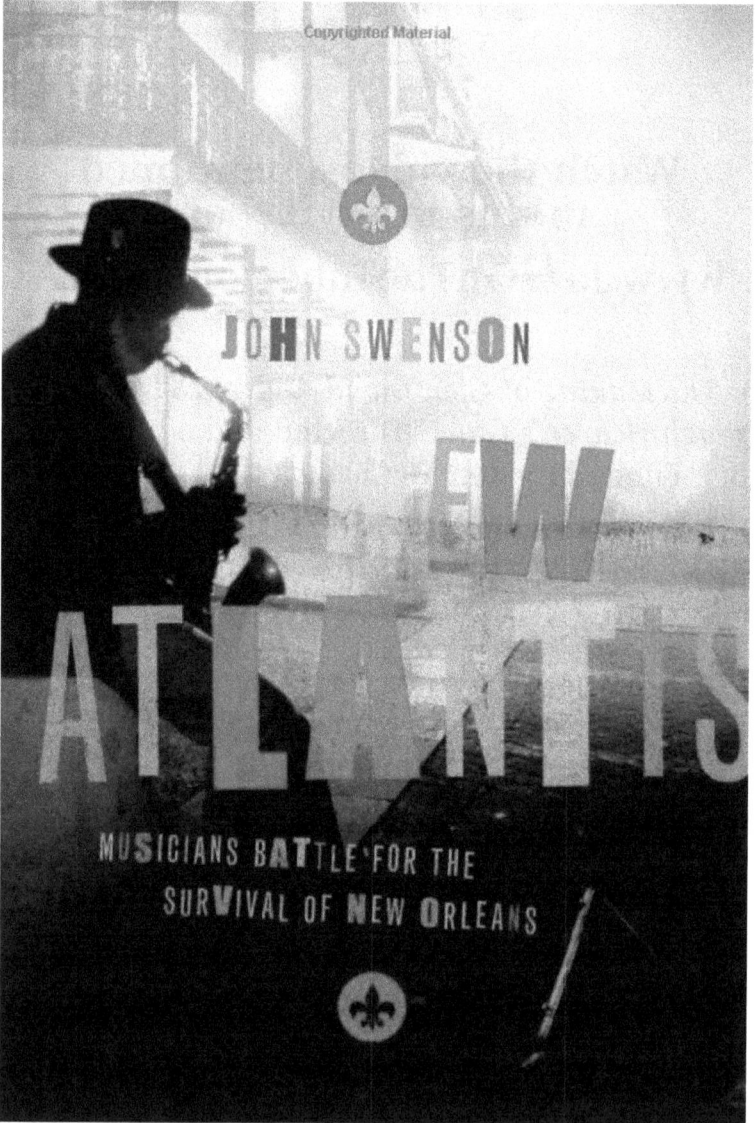

JOHN SWENSON

NEW ATLANTIS

MUSICIANS BATTLE FOR THE
SURVIVAL OF NEW ORLEANS

Swenson, John. *New Atlantis: Musicians Battle For The Survival Of New Orleans.* Oxford University Press, 2011.

Praise for *New Atlantis*

"I thank John Swenson for writing the book that not only brings New Orleans music up-to-date, but illustrates in no uncertain terms the sacrifice and tenaciousness it takes to be a musician in New Orleans. Best of all, Swenson also captures in great detail the joy and comeraderie each musician feels when he/she plays and the bond created with the audience to create a live music experience like no other. Having lived and worked in the New Orleans music biz arena, reading New Atlantis was like reading a letter from home. Juicy details and thoughtful commentary in a well-written ode to the glue that keeps New Orleans viable and growing."

- From a review by Kathleen Rippey

GLEN DAVID ANDREWS

Excerpts from his speech
at the "Silence Is Violence rally"
Recorded January 11, 2007

"You see all the young black people right here? We preserve New Orleans' history and music all over the world. Not all of us is murderers. I don't have no ambition on going to Angola for the rodeo, for a video, or nothing else. I don't go around talking about people.

See all these people right here, ain't none of us over thirty and we're all making a statement for young black people. We're going to walk in the steps of Tuba Fats."

...

"We're tired of y'all coming to the second line with them guns. If you're not coming to dance stay the hell away from there. Straight up."

...

"And I'm going to make this statement, and I'm very serious. I'm scared to death of the police. I'm going to tell you that straight up. Just the other day I'm coming from Preservation Hall, and the first said, "Hey you, come here."

Can't you see I got on a black suit with a horn? Do it look like I'm selling rocks? Do I look like I'm trying to rob somebody? I'm going to sit down and sing traditional jazz."

...

"If we don't get music in schools, then first of all, people, stop having this mentality where nobody can't tell your child nothing. If nobody can't tell your child nothing then go back to Houston. I don't like Houston anyway, I love New Orleans. I don't like Atlanta, I love New Orleans. I don't like Tennessee, I love New Orleans. We're going to stand united.

This is a shame for this woman [mother of Dinerral Shavers] to have to be up here. This is a shame, where children don't know nothing but "nigga" this and "nigga" that. I ain't no nigga and I don't know no niggas. I don't know no crackers or no honkies. All I know is citizens of New Orleans. And if you ain't going to be a citizen of New Orleans, get the hell away from us.

I live in a trailer and the only thing that keeps my neighborhood going is John Blanchard from the Rock 'n' Bowl, whose help provides extra security up there. [Addressed to city officials:] It's too damn dark, man. Get on your job, we need lights. The bus don't run at night, well how the hell am I going to get home? You're talking about starting a curfew? My gig don't get over till 2:30 am. Which is going to cut my money."

Watch these related videos at: www.JazzOnTheTube.com/NOLA

(1) *Glen David Andrews at the "Silence Is Violence rally" at City Hall, New Orleans.* (2007)

(2) *Glen David Andrews, "Easter Sunday Parking Lot Jam."* (2009) Filmed by Ken McCarthy.

Ronald Lewis and The House of Dance & Feathers

Ronald Lewis (1951-2020)
in conversation with Chuck Perkins
Recorded in 2009

Chuck Perkins: Right now we are on the other side of town, all the way downtown, in the Lower Ninth Ward at 1317 Tupelo Street at the House of Dance & Feathers. And right now we have the very esteemed Mr. Ronald Lewis, the curator of The House of Dance & Feathers. And I'll let you hear a little bit from Mr. Lewis.

Ronald Lewis: Thank you for coming here, Chuck. Because I always like to have people come here who want to continue telling our story - from '05 up to now, and what it's going to take to bring our city back, and the various parts of our community. What I experienced, on the good side, is how people embraced what I was doing. As I spoke on TV talking about the rebuilding of my community, and how we weren't going to give up the land. People had something to connect to. So what they did was they started bringing items here. A lady brought a washboard to me that came from a man who was 96 years old.

One of my grandchildren's uncle's, those cold drinks and bleach bottles over there, he dug them up at Audubon Park during some excavating. And you know, they got many moons on them. People feel that this is ours. We got something to connect to.

I used this to keep our message out there about the rebuilding of the Lower Nine, and how we had nearly 70% homeownership down here. And when the world heard about it, they said "That many black people own homes?" And we say, yes. Our people came off of the sugarcane plantations and came out of these cotton fields and they bought land in the big city of New Orleans. Very cheap. And it brought a quality of life down here that was different from across the city. I'm a product of this. This is why I proudly say that our community is going to rebuild, one house and one family at a time. And I use the culture, which is the fabric of our life here in the city of New Orleans, as the vehicle to put the message out.

Life After Katrina

Ronald Lewis: We have growth. It's slow growth. When everybody left here, they would look to be gone for two or three days. Now it's gone into four years, and over 100,000 of our people are still not back in the city of New Orleans. So those who are migrating back are finding a way to rebuild their lives, and they're making it happen. And our city is being rebuilt off the back of the people who love this city.

Chuck Perkins: That's right.

Ronald Lewis: Not the people who are the Chambers of Commerce or whatever, but the people who will go out there to the second line, the people who go to the various festivals here in the city, and just do the everyday things that we love. For my community, I always tell people one house and one family at a time, because the Lower Ninth Ward was the tsunami of the United States.

Chuck Perkins: It was the epicenter.

Ronald Lewis: When that water came through here, my home had 14 feet of water. Up to the rooftop. I lost everything that me and my wife had accumulated over that 30-plus years. And with everybody being in the same boat, we've just been picking up each other and trying to make it happen. Brad Pitt got his Make It Right program. Then they got the Global Green Project down here. And I'm championing a cause, the Musicians' Village over there on an old school site. We got an old school site here in the Lower Nine. Wouldn't that habitat have a great impact, if they crossed this ward?

Chuck Perkins: I gotcha.

Ronald Lewis: And provide affordable housing for people of this community to come back. I tell people, the streets of New Orleans talk to you. Because we live in the streets of New Orleans. Our home is our bedding place. But we get out of them villas every chance we get. Whether it's a barbecue in the yard, following a second line, or just going to some other social events. And you feel that. You feel the people embracing each other all the time. And using these New Orleans events as a gathering point.

Second Lines

Ronald Lewis: Many people come into my museum who grew up in New Orleans, who lived in the Garden District, who lived in Marigny, and had never been to a second line... What they tell me is what their grandparents and their parents told them about when they went to the Zulu parade. It was something that wasn't talked about, but it was done. You know, because it was like being taboo. But these next generations who are coming out, they're being like Columbus, and they done "discovered" the second line. [Laughing.]

Chuck Perkins: Right.

Ronald Lewis: And now here they are.

Chuck Perkins: And they realize how wonderful it is.

Ronald Lewis: That's right. Yes, it's our creation, but it's a people's event. With the House of Dance & Feathers, I incorporated my life in the culture. From being president of the Big Nine Social and Pleasure Club to being a former Mardi Gras Indian saint.

I took the House of Dance & Feathers and made it a cultural education center for those who want to come here and want to know the truth. Because all these cultural anthropologists come to New Orleans, they be Columbus and done "discovered" a rare culture in the city of New Orleans that's been here existing. And then they want to write about it. And fortunately, my book that just came out, gives you an insightful perspective about this great culture, why we do it, and why it's so embedded in our life. We're a hands-on people.

When you see the streamers, as we call them, the parade fans and the umbrellas and all of that, it's because we like to create, we like to put our hands on things and say, "Look at us."

When you look at that history - through the Caribbean, through Latin America, all the way back to the African coast - everything came through here. When you look at the North Side Skull and Bones, you're looking at tradition in Haiti, you're looking at tradition in Africa. When you look at the umbrellas of the Ivory Coast when the chiefs come out on a certain day and wear one color and everybody in the tribe wears that color. And they made these beautiful umbrellas with symbols on top that have some representation. Well, you find this right here in the city of New Orleans.

Because we are the most African city in the United States of America. We are descendants of the people that came off of those slave ships, that brought all this food and culture and everything to the city. So through that, when people first come here, the first thing they say is, "I've seen this somewhere." And as they go back, they realize when they were in the Caribbean and saw street festivals or parades in Cuba, then they have that connection. And that connection is those boats that came through that passage to get to the port city of New Orleans.

Mardi Gras Indians

Chuck Perkins: Let me ask you this question right here. You were a Mardi Gras Indian as well?

Ronald Lewis: Yes.

Chuck Perkins: Mardi Gras, for Mardi Gras Indians, that's a big thing.

Ronald Lewis: Yeah. That's the day that we put all that effort and money that we don't have into making one of them costumes, to walk out your door, and for the people in your neighborhood to tell you what beautiful work you'd done.

Chuck Perkins: And that's what I wanted to ask. I'm going to assume some people listening don't know anything about Mardi Gras Indians. Take me through it, step by step. I guess the first thing starts with you getting your suit together and then all the way to Mardi Gras and what you do that day.

Ronald Lewis: I'll tell you what. This right here [points to drawing] is the beginning of a Mardi Gras Indian suit. From that first idea you have of how you want to design the suit. And from you creating that first image, then you move from there to fill in the blanks. And filling in the blanks...

Chuck Perkins: So I guess on this one, you started doing it...

Ronald Lewis: Right.

Chuck Perkins: So how do you get the beads on there?

Ronald Lewis: With a thread and needle. It is a passion. When you turn it around [turns the piece around].

Chuck Perkins: Oh, I see.

Ronald Lewis: Yes. The almighty thread and needle.

Chuck Perkins: Is there a patch like this that's completely done? Let's hold it up right next to each other.

Ronald Lewis: I'm gonna show you my book cover.

Chuck Perkins: Oh, that's the cover.

Ronald Lewis: That's the cover of my book.

Chuck Perkins: What's the time involved for this?

Ronald Lewis: Well, it's your commitment. "I've got to get this piece finished."

Chuck Perkins: About how much time do think it would take to do this?

Ronald Lewis: If you were serious. A month.

Chuck Perkins: Just for this part right here?

Ronald Lewis: Just to do this.

Chuck Perkins: Okay. Now for this one, right here?

Ronald Lewis: For this serious beading, it would take about a month, a month and a half. But see this particular piece here... I feel like, just like any artist, there's one piece that is your signature piece of work. I did this piece in 1992, which took me about five months...

Chuck Perkins: Wow. Just for this one piece?

Ronald Lewis: Yes. Because it was so intricate. And, you know, all this is vision. I had visions of the colors that I wanted in it. I had to go out and find these colors of beads and get certain parts started. The vision and the spirit takes control of you, then you end up with this.

Chuck Perkins: So for this suit in 1992, let's assume that the Mardi Gras was going to be in February. When would you start working on this suit, at what time?

Ronald Lewis: I start like maybe in March.

Chuck Perkins: So you got a good 11-month run.

Ronald Lewis: That's right. It's a commitment. When you say it's a commitment that means your financial commitment, your time involved. I was working for the transit system on the streetcar tracks. When I got off out of that grit and dirt, I would come home, take a shower, eat, and sew till two or three o'clock in the morning, and had to be to work at six o'clock. That was a commitment of completion for the target date of Mardi Gras day. And while I'm working on a piece, I got other friends who work on pieces for me. And say a month before Mardi Gras we start bringing all this stuff together and make it happen.

Chuck Perkins: Okay, so about a month, that's when you start bringing the feathers and everything.

Ronald Lewis: Right.

Chuck Perkins: I was never a Mardi Gras Indian, even though I love the culture. The only reference I have is maybe something like Christmas. You know, as a kid, on Christmas Day I can hardly sleep at night. Or even a big football game, you get that same kind of rush.

Ronald Lewis: Oh, it's such a rush for you to walk out of that door, and you done put all this together. You're saying to yourself your work is beautiful. But to see when you're standing out there and all these people with their children and everybody saying, "Oh, look how beautiful you are. It's a great job you've done." And then that feeding-off-the-people energy is what brings you into that ritual battle of walking five and six miles with all this weight on. Just to tell that next Mardi Gras Indian, "You didn't do your homework."

Social Aid and Pleasure Clubs

Chuck Perkins: Explain to people what social aid and pleasure clubs are.

Ronald Lewis: It goes back to our benevolent

societies here in the city of New Orleans. With the Young Men Olympians, it's the oldest parade benevolent in the city of New Orleans, well over 120 years. And what the benevolent did out of the church was serve the community. And if you belonged to the benevolent, then you had a chance to have an honorable burial. Because the benevolent had burial plots. And they served the community through social aid, trying to help feed families and doing whatever. It changed over time, from the benevolent to the social aid and pleasure club, which was more festive. Benevolents wore their black and white, put on their parade, and went back to the church. We still hold the church in high regard, but once we get our blessing, then we bring on the big party. We stop at every happy spot and get happy, and the followers get happy. And when those four hours are over, everybody's happy.

Chuck Perkins: Everybody's happy.

Ronald Lewis: Yes.

Chuck Perkins: So you've been a Mardi Gras Indian, and you've been a member of the social aid and pleasure club. Did you start the Big Nine?

Ronald Lewis: I helped found it.

Chuck Perkins: You helped found it. In terms of getting ready for one of those big events as a Mardi Gras Indian, getting ready for that big parade, with the Big Nine that's going to march across that canal. Are there similarities and differences?

Ronald Lewis: The similarity is the preparing. But

what makes the difference, making the Mardi Gras Indian suit is an individual thing. Whereas preparing for your parade and your group is a group thing, as a whole. You've got to determine the clothes you're going to wear and get everybody to agree upon that color, and all of that, and then put the whole batch together.

Chuck Perkins: Boy, I betcha getting twenty dudes to agree on the same color suit might not be as easy as it seems.

Ronald Lewis: Let me tell you, sometimes you have to become a dictator for the best interest of the club. You just have to say: "I'm cutting it off here and this is what we're going to do. Now pay your parade taxes and everything, and let the show go on." But that's New Orleans. Like I was saying, when the social aid and pleasure clubs took over, we still do social things, except now we're using the events of our modern times. Book and school supply giveaways, giving out food baskets and these sorts of things and making social statements. We're not just a party group.

When you look at the House of Dance & Feathers, you come to a whole table of educational literature. Letting people know, yes, we made these great costumes, and we dance on the street, but look at here, look at the education that sits on this table. When you come in here, you're going to look at all this great stuff. Then you're going to end up right over here saying I didn't know about this. And this is what the House of Dance & Feathers does. It's an education center.

The Book

Chuck Perkins: I have the book that Mr. Lewis is talking about right here, *The House of Dance & Feathers*, and it's the real deal. I had a chance to look through it, and if you are interested in the culture of New Orleans, Mardi Gras Indians, social aid and pleasure clubs, and the Skull and Bone Gang, I highly recommend getting this book right here.

Ronald Lewis: Finally, a book came from the inside, a person who lived this entire culture. And this is what people feel who looked in the book, who read the book, say, "Oh, we never had a book so in-depth about our cultural life." And like I tell people, it's not my book, it's the people's book. That's why I'm honored for y'all to come here and to be a messenger.

Watch the video of this interview at: www.JazzOnTheTube.com/NOLA

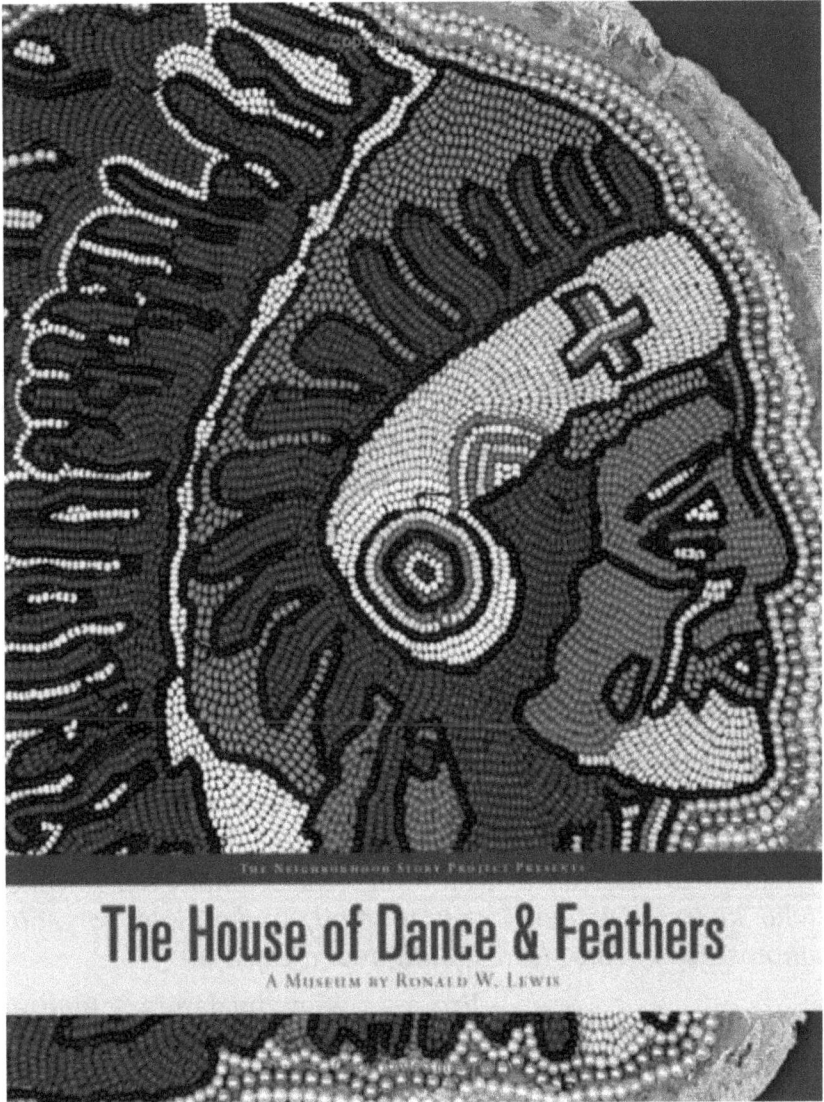

The House of Dance & Feathers

A MUSEUM BY RONALD W. LEWIS

Lewis, Ronald. *The House of Dance & Feathers*. UNO Press/
Neighborhood Story Project, 2009.

Praise for The House of Dance & Feathers

"I spent the first 4th of July after Katrina in Ronald's driveway in the completely devastated Lower 9th Ward. It was me, Rachel, Dan, Abram, Ronald, Ronald's family and a bunch of architecture students from Kansas - grilling in the rain and playing cards in the gutted frame of a house with a tarp for a roof. There was not a house with the lights on for miles in any direction. Every once in a while, a neighbor would drive by, and Ronald would go out and tell them that everyone was here to help him build a museum and that they should move back because the neighborhood was going to rise from the wreckage.

This book helps me understand how he was able to convince folks, and why people came to him for convincing. The stories, photos and soul in this book, and the care with which it was put together: Amazing. It's so hard to explain to people what New Orleans and second lines and Mardi Gras mean, now I have an amazing tool to help in my explaining.

Inspirational on a deep level, educational even to folks who know NOLA well, fun to read, and full of gorgeous photos. Every American should own a copy."

- From a review by Jamie Schweser

Growing up in New Orleans & the Lower Ninth Ward

Roger Lewis in Conversation with Ken McCarthy
Recorded in 2020

Ken McCarthy: Today, we're going to be talking with a distinguished musical professor from the land down south of New Orleans.

I want to say something about New Orleans before we get started. To me, it's a big dividing line in the jazz world. There are people that have never been to New Orleans, and all they really know about New Orleans is Louis Armstrong, and "that's where jazz began." And that's good. That's the story. Then there are people that have been there as tourists that maybe have gone in for a couple of days and seen Bourbon Street and come home. And that's good. But it's a little bit like going to Times Square and thinking you know New York. There's a lot more to it. Then there are people that go to a Jazz Fest, and then spend a week or more and go to all the performances, and that's good.

But my experience with New Orleans is that it's like a big onion. You peel away one layer, and you think you understand it, and then you realize, oh, no, there's more to it. And then you peel away another layer. And there's more to it. And finally, at one point, it finally dawns on you, you're never ever going to get to the bottom of it. There's so much there.

Today, we're going to look at one piece through the eyes of one musician and his life and his career. And we're only going to be able to scratch the surface of his music. And that's just scratching the surface of New Orleans. So I give this introduction because I want to make sure that everybody who loves this music, as soon as this crazy thing that we're going through is over, get on a plane, go to New Orleans and experience it firsthand. Go to all the clubs, and have the musical experience of your life. So with that as an introduction, welcome, Roger Lewis.

Roger Lewis: How are you doing?

Ken McCarthy: I'm doing good, thank you.

Roger Lewis: How's everybody doing out there in the world?

Ken McCarthy: Well, I think we're all doing better than the newspaper tells us. But that's another story. There are so many things I'd like to talk about with you. I have a long, long set of notes. But the first thing I want to say to everybody is, if you don't know the Dirty Dozen Brass Band, now you know the name, you should absolutely check it out. They have a website, DirtyDozenBrassBand.com. They have a Facebook page, of course.

Maybe we'll start there, to give people a sense of this organization and how important it is to world music. I think everybody knows there's a brass band tradition in New Orleans. And everybody probably, at this point, has heard some of the modern brass bands. But what we don't know about is that transition. How did it go from traditional to what we're hearing today, which is multifaceted and multidimensional? Roger, you and your friends at the Dirty Dozen Brass Band played a big role in the transformation, the evolution, or the development, of the brass band. Can you talk a little bit about what was going on when you guys got together and said, "Let's do something different with the brass band configuration"? What was going on in New Orleans at the time?

Roger Lewis: At the time we started, most of the brass bands were playing traditional New Orleans music. Like hymns that they play in the church, and you speed them up when you hit the streets, music like that, and march music like "Bugle Boy March."

When we started, we were playing traditional New Orleans music. But in the Dirty Dozen Brass Band you have the opportunity to play whatever kind of music you want to play. And we just were trying to play the music that we wanted to play. So we started playing the music of Michael Jackson. We started playing the music of Duke Ellington and Charlie Parker, and Horace Silver, Dizzy Gillespie, Thelonious Monk. And we brought this music to the streets of New Orleans, with a different beat. Not trying to change New Orleans music, you know. And playing a lot of fusion, and of course our own compositions, we play a lot of original music also.

We brought this music to the streets, like going down the street playing "Blue Monk." People dancing all for that. "Bongo Beep", "Caravan", "Chippin'." And we made up a song called "My Feet Can't Fail Me Now." Matter of fact, that was our first CD in the George Wein Collection on Concord Records.

In "Feet Can't Fail Me Now" you have the music of Charlie Parker, and also at the very end you have the music of Horace Silver, and other little things in between. And we slightly picked up the beat, because the New Orleans traditional music is like, it's not too fast and it's not too slow. It's like in between, you can dance slow or could dance way up. But we picked the beat way up. So they actually created a dance, what they call buck jumping.

I always say, we used to do these four-hour second line parades, I would always say when you come to the second line that the Dirty Dozen is playing you better have your tennis shoes and your jogging shoes, you're gonna have a good workout. You're gonna lose a couple of pounds because for four hours the music is gonna be intense. We're kind of credited with changing the history of brass band music.

Kirk Joseph, which is our sousaphone player, his style of playing kind of revolutionized that kind of music, brass band music. But there was a guy before Kirk Joseph, his name was Anthony Lacen, better known as Tuba Fats, who played with the Olympia Brass Band. Now, the Olympia Brass Band probably was the first band I heard, the great Olympia Brass

Band. Those guys probably came with the funk, you know, I'd say even before the Dirty Dozen had the funk. They started interjecting all these contemporary avant-garde sounds, and the music of Charlie Parker.

Interweaving this music with what we were doing caught the ear of a very famous producer by the name of George Wein. We were playing at a McDonogh School in the French Quarter and he heard the band and he invited us to record on Concord on the George Wein Collection, which we did. That was our first - well, it wasn't our first CD but it was our first, I would say, international label.

And then we got a booking agent. Between those two guys, they put us on all these jazz concerts all over the world. So we got a chance to play with and opened up for, a lot of famous jazz musicians. And then eventually started headlining our own shows. So that's pretty much how we got started.

The band's been together for over 40-odd years. We started traveling in '83, I think. But we started playing, putting the band together in 1976.

Now, I don't want to leave out the guy who really started the band. His name was Benny Jones. Benny Jones is a drummer. He also started the Treme Brass Band, and he started the Chosen Few Brass Band. You know, Benny Jones was the guy who really started, at that time it was called Original Sixth Ward Dirty Dozen Brass Band, back in '76 when he started this band. Of course, he's no longer a member because the band has changed. Different personnel over the years. When we first started, Benny Jones, Jenell Marshall, then when Benny Jones left the band it was Lionel Batiste Jr. And of course, Kirk Joseph and Charles Joseph, brothers. Gregory Davis, Kevin Harris, Efrem Towns, and myself Roger Lewis. And it was an all-acoustic band. But as the years went by, we added guitar, and at one point we had a full rhythm section. We had Richard Knox and Carl LeBlanc. And then Jake Eckert and Jamie McLean. And different drummers, Terence Higgins. Then we converted into a set drummer, you know, Terrence Higgins and Jermal Watson. And the list goes on, I'm trying to remember all these people. Another guy Kyle Roussel, and Fred Sanders, keyboard players. So the band changed. As the band is today, it's Julian Addison on drums, he's from Dayton, Ohio.

Ken McCarthy: So when people are out there all over the world and hearing all these interesting, exciting local brass bands, they should know that, of course, it started in New Orleans, but also that it started with the Dirty Dozen, and of course, as you mentioned the Olympia Brass Band. They've been around since the beginning of time, haven't they?

Roger Lewis: Oh, yeah. The Olympia. We had the Onward Brass Band, we had the Eureka Brass Band. Some of the older brass bands, we had the Tornadoes Brass Band. I mean, these are older bands before the Dirty Dozen.

Now a lot of people say the brass band thing was dying out. That's not true. They've always had brass bands in New Orleans. The only thing that happened was the Dirty Dozen came along and changed everything. Not trying to. People think it was a calculated plan, but it wasn't a calculated plan to do what we did. We just wanted to play the music we wanted to play.

I was studying music at university under the direction of Edward "Kidd" Jordan. You know I'm the oldest guy in the band. I've been playing music 60 some-odd years. I'm 79 years old. I'm the oldest guy in everybody's band, pretty much [Laughs]. I play with another group called Delfeayo Marsalis & the Uptown Jazz Orchestra. That's my big band gig that I do when I'm not doing Dirty Dozen. But I've been playing music for a long time, so I brought a lot of history to the band. The other guys, whatever music they wanted to play, or if they had an original composition, just bring it to the band, and work on it and get it played, and we play it. Unselfishly. That attitude made the difference with us because we were experimenting with a lot of different music, different sounds, avant-garde, everything.

Ken McCarthy: I think some people are maybe not aware that New Orleans is not a Pharaoh's tomb. In other words, it's alive. People are always influenced by new things. They're listening. When Charlie Parker was around, people in New Orleans were listening to Charlie Parker.

Roger Lewis: There were people in New Orleans who were playing like Charlie Parker, like George 'Son' Johnson. You know Charlie Parker wasn't the only cat that was playing like that. There were people in New Orleans that was playing like that.

When I first went on the road, on an international tour, I joined the Fats Domino band in 1971. I played with him until he played his last gig. It's a whole history, playing with Fats Domino, Dave Bartholomew, and the great Lee Allen and Herbert Hardesty. Herbert Hardesty was the guy playing all the solos on Fats Domino records. He passed a few years ago. And the great Lee Allen, who was the saxophone player on almost all R&B and rock and roll records. He was the tenor player on Little Richard. He was the tenor saxophone player that played all the solos.

And as matter of fact, since we're talking about that, even back in the day New Orleans was not only jazz, but New Orleans was a rhythm and blues town. Fats Domino, he would tell you, we don't call our music rock and roll, as far as I knew he was playing rhythm and blues. Rock and roll came from somewhere else, but New Orleans was a rhythm and blues town. And at one time, New Orleans was like Motown. Everybody was coming to New Orleans to record. Sometimes people get it mixed up. New Orleans is not just a jazz town, New Orleans is a melting pot of different styles of music. We're influenced by the French, the Italians, we've got all different cultures here in New Orleans. You got a little bit of everything in New Orleans music.

Ken McCarthy: You did a show with Jon Cleary on his live stream, which was great.

Roger Lewis: Yeah, we were just getting warmed up. We had a bad connection when we first started doing the interview. And then we took a little break. And then maybe the last 15 minutes of the interview, we start really getting into it, you know? Because he wanted to know how New Orleans was during the time I was coming up, as far as the music scene and places that were around.

Ken McCarthy: Yeah, that's what I felt. And I was like, "Oh, I've got to follow this thread because there's some interesting stuff there." Let me ask you about something that came up in that call that'll lead us to talking about the New Orleans scene. You mentioned that there were guys who were in New Orleans playing like Charlie Parker. I'm gonna guess they weren't copying Charlie Parker. They discovered it on their own...

Roger Lewis: They were playing their style, man... playing their style of music. Man, we had so many great saxophone players around here. They had a dude by the name of Nat Perrilliat. When John Coltrane came to New Orleans, he was playing at a club called Vernon's Lounge. As soon as Trane got off the plane he was looking for Nat Perrilliat. Nat Perrilliat was a great saxophonist. As a matter of fact, he was in that league with John Coltrane.

They had a guy around here by the name of Eddie Williams. He could play everything John Coltrane could play. Oh man, we've had so many great sax players.

I was saying earlier, when I joined the Fats Domino band in 1971. We went all over the world. I went all over the world with him, and I got a chance to hear the best of the best. And I said, "Man, they got dudes at home that sound like this. I've been hearing this all my life."

There was a guy by the name of Alvin "Red" Tyler. Now, Alvin "Red" Tyler was a saxophonist. He actually was a famous guy because he was a studio musician, and he was one of the guys who was on all of those early rhythm and blues records, including Little Richard. He was a studio musician at Cosimo Matassa's studio where Little Richard recorded. But he was the first guy I heard play jazz live. When I heard him, he was playing tenor sax. I was hanging out with a guy by the name of Frederic Kemp. Now that guy there, he was a great saxophonist.

There are a lot of people that you don't hear about that don't make it to the forefront. We got musicians, man, that you probably never heard of. Man, New Orleans has so many Jazz musicians that can play. And New Orleans was a drummer's heaven, man. The difference with New Orleans music is the beat. It's that beat.

The other thing is that people are steady flocking to New Orleans to find out how to play New Orleans music, but what they don't realize is New Orleans music is very spiritual. Because a lot of musicians come out of the church, and they got the Gospel in their music. And a lot of guys play fast and play a lot of notes, but those notes don't, you know, no disrespect to education in music, period. But if you can't feel, it don't make sense. Music is a feeling, man. It's how you make people feel.

Ken McCarthy: Which raises the issue of the church, and the importance of church in New Orleans, and how many New Orleans musicians really got their education, their foundation in church, first hearing it as small children.

Roger Lewis: Well, there's a ballroom on the corner, and there's a church on the corner. But most people come up in the church, you know, you get up in the morning on Sunday, you go to Sunday school, during the week you go to prayer service.

New Orleans is very spiritual. It used to be, back in my generation, your mother make you go to church. And a lot of people come up playing in the church.

Like there's a guy by the name of Danny Barker who created the Fairview Baptist Band. So a lot of those guys came up, guys like Leroy Jones, Gregg Stafford, and all these different cats, come out the church.

What I'm saying is the Gospel is in the music of New Orleans. People try to figure out what it is, it's the Gospel. That's the difference. It ain't about nobody playing all them thousands of notes. It's how the music feels. That's why they come here to try to figure it out. That's what made Louis Armstrong so great. And Sidney Bechet, and Mahalia Jackson, you know what I mean? There are a lot of elements in New Orleans music to make New Orleans music what it is. That's why people flocking here to find out what's happening.

And then that's why, when you go to other places and play this music, it's so well accepted all over the world. We have a lot of great musicians like Wynton Marsalis, Delfeayo Marsalis, Branford Marsalis, Nicholas Payton, Terence Blanchard, and all these cats. When they left New Orleans they just excelled, man, to higher levels. Because it's something else.

Ken McCarthy: That's why I always encourage people who love music, if they have never been, they really need to go to New Orleans. It's another world. There's a quote somewhere, it's even on video. I'm going to see if I can find it, where Louis Armstrong is saying "It's the ladies in church that drove the music, they'd get to rocking..." and he considered that the basis of the music. That's pretty deep. So in your era, when you were growing up, the church was a lot more solid, more people were involved in it, and it really held the communities together, more than today.

Roger Lewis: You had the church, and then you had what would be called benevolent society groups. Benevolent society groups were clubs where if you didn't have money to bury a loved one or money to take care of your family, or you needed a little help, they would come to your aid. Then later on they degraded into what we call social and pleasure clubs.

Ken McCarthy: And each one of these groups has music at the heart of it. If there is going to be an event, they're going to have a live band, it's going to be a brass band.

Roger Lewis: Oh yeah.

Ken McCarthy: They're all going to have their annual parade or their second line. They're all going to have their annual ball to raise money for the parade. It's unusual in America, it's such a live musical city. You can't do anything significant in New Orleans without having a live band involved.

Roger Lewis: They might have an event where they have a rhythm and blues band playing, then they hire a brass band to come in at the last part of the gig. The brass band comes in and just the energy and the feeling of what it is, it's totally different.

Just like when the Dirty Dozen used to open up for people. And a lot of people didn't want to play after us because we would just turn the place out. I remember recently, I think it was in Germany, we did about five or six encores. And I think the Buddy Rich Big Band was coming on after us. We did about five or six encores, and people would not let us leave man. It was unreal.

The impact of the music and the feeling of the music is just totally different. It's a different thing. My wife Mari Watanabe, she came from Tokyo, Japan to learn New Orleans traditional jazz. She probably knows more about New Orleans's traditional jazz than most people that live here. She studied styles of the likes of Sweet Emma, a player at Preservation Hall, and the style of James Booker; she can play like these people. I'm just saying that's the impact that the music of this city has on people.

Even back in the day when Motown took a lot of people out of New Orleans and brought them to Motown, like Smokey Johnson, Earl King, and all these cats that were happening at the time, back in the late '50s early '60s. New Orleans drummers are the most sought-after drummers. You got people like Herlin Riley, who's probably one of the most sought-after jazz musicians. And then you had the great Earl Palmer, who had drums in everybody's studio in Hollywood, who recorded with everybody. [Editor's note: Palmer, a member of the Rock and Roll Hall of Fame, moved to LA where he became a member of The Wrecking Crew, laying down studio tracks for Frank Sinatra, Phil Spector, Ray Charles, Sam Cooke, Ritchie Valens, The Beach Boys, Neil Young, and many others.]

Ken McCarthy: People may not know those names, but they've heard the music, but behind a frontliner, somebody who has the big name, but the guy playing the drums, you may not know who it was.

Roger Lewis: Even in the Ray Charles band. Charles Otis, better known as Honeyboy, I mean the list goes on and on. I'm talking about Clarence Johnston, John Boudreaux, and cats like that. These cats were great New Orleans drummers, man. David

Lee played with Sonny Rollins at one time. New Orleans is like a drummer's paradise.

Ken McCarthy: I looked at the numbers. I don't think New Orleans ever has had more than a million people total living in it, but when you look at the impact that this relatively small place has had on the music of the world, it's outsized. It's like a boxer punching above his weight. It's almost crazy. The only other place I can think of that's comparable is Cuba. But Cuba's got 11 million people. So they have 10 times as many people. But I don't know any other place on earth that has produced more master musicians in the last 100 years. I just don't think there's one that's come close.

Roger Lewis: It's a musical town, it's a musical spiritual town. There's no place on the planet like this city.

Ken McCarthy: You mentioned Ray Charles, and here's something I'd like to talk about. There are a lot of famous musicians who had a big impression left on them from visiting or living in New Orleans that people just aren't aware of. One of them is Ray Charles. Another one that nobody ever talks about is Lester Young. He spent part of his childhood in New Orleans, chasing after the bands and listening to all the music. That had to have an influence. And then the other one, I really would love to talk about is Ornette. We have a whole section on Ornette on the Jazz on the Tube website because he was a friend of mine.[1]

---

1   See Appendix - Ornette Coleman (2)

Roger Lewis: Ornette Coleman?

Ken McCarthy: Yeah. Now, people don't realize it, but Ornette came to New Orleans I think when he was 19, and he stayed with the Lastie family.

Roger Lewis: Guess what? I lived in the 1900 block of Delery. The Lasties lived in the 1800 block. And when I was a kid I used to hear those guys - the house they lived in was like a camelback house. You know what a camelback is?

Ken McCarthy: It's got a little front and a big back?

Roger Lewis: It's got like a camelback, it's a flat house with an upstairs in the back. Anyway, them cats used to be back up in there, and I used to hear them playing, practicing back then when I was a little kid. I was kind of shy. I should have knocked on the door. But Ornette Coleman and the Lasties, David Lastie, Melvin Lastie, Walter Lastie, Charles Otis. All of them cats would be back there practicing, man. He spent a lot of time with the Lasties back then. I didn't have a chance to meet him.

Ken McCarthy: My understanding is that the Lasties' home was a refuge for musicians. They took care of Ornette. He got stranded on the road and I think he lived with them for months.

Roger Lewis: Yeah, it was a great family. It was a musical family. Their grandfather, I think he's credited with introducing the drums to the church, Frank Lastie. His grandson is Herlin Riley.

Ken McCarthy: Oh really?

Roger Lewis: Yeah, a lot of people don't know, but Herlin Riley was a trumpet player. He always played the drums. But at 12 years old, he played his first gig with me, I think it was at Lawless Elementary School. His uncle came by my house and said, "Come on out. We doing something for the kids. Play a couple of numbers." I'm on stage and Herlin comes in, comes up on stage, little kid with a trumpet. And man this cat was playing like a pro. I was like, "How can he play like that? I'm trying to play those notes." And his uncle was laughing at me because I didn't know what was happening. But his other uncle Melvin Lastie taught him how to play the trumpet.

Boy, he was a hell of a little trumpet player, man. He didn't pursue it. I think he had some kind of stuff with his chops. I don't know but then when I saw him again he was playing with Ahmad Jamal, he was playing drums. I was wondering how that happened, but he told me, he said, man, we always did play the drums. So the story goes, when they were sitting at the dinner table because his grandfather was a drummer, Frank Lastie, they would be playing rhythms with the knives and forks and stuff. A lot of people get started like that. It's just everybody in everybody's family plays some kind of musical instrument, or has played some kind of musical instrument. That's why it's such a musical city.

Ken McCarthy: My understanding is Frank Lastie inherited a powerful spiritual tradition. He was a disciple of Mother Catherine Seals of the Spiritualist church. In the 1920s, she invited him to bring his drumset into the church, the first time that was ever done in New Orleans. [Editor's note: Another of Frank Lastie's claims to fame, in addition to raising a family of master musicians, was that he was a member of the Waif's Home Band (Milnes Boys Home) where he played alongside young Louis Armstrong.]

Roger Lewis: He had a church down in the Ninth Ward. He had his own church. [Editor's Note: The Guiding Star Spiritual Church.]

Ken McCarthy: When I was talking with Ornette about life in the Lower Nine, he was older at that time and he didn't remember too many details. But one thing he said, and maybe you could help us because you were there. I only know the Lower Nine after Katrina, right, so I don't know anything. He told me the Lower Nine was like the countryside. There were trees and gardens. Tell us about what it looked like and what life was like in the Lower Nine.

Roger Lewis: Alright, I'm gonna tell you. I was raised uptown in what we call the Garden District. I was raised on Camp between Pleasant and Harmony. How about that? Then my parents moved to the Irish Channel, where all the Irish people lived, which is on the other side of the dividing line, Magazine Street. And I lived on Seventh and Tchoupitoulas. Now Tchoupitoulas is the last street in the city going that way. My dad bought a little piece of property down in the Lower Ninth Ward on Delery Street, actually, it's a little short street that runs about two or three blocks, behind Delery Street, but it's very short. Delery Street is the last street before you get into St. Bernard Parish, which is the last street in the city. From one extreme to the other. Now when we moved down to the Ninth Ward, they didn't have paved streets. Might have had one paved street, St. Maurice. But everything else was like country. They had what we call gutters, like a ditch. Everybody had what they call septic tanks in their yard because we didn't have sewage and all that stuff back then. So that was country, man. People had chickens, horses, and a lot of greens. It was the country.

Ken McCarthy: That's what Ornette said, he said there were a lot of trees and leaves.

Roger Lewis: Yeah, and I tell you what, standard shoe apparel was you better have you some galoshes because when it rained... I remember when I was a kid we used to have planks. We'd put planks leading up to the house from the street. We didn't have paved sidewalks or none of that stuff. It was the country.

And they only had two buses. I'm going back to my childhood. There was, on St. Claude Street, St. Claude Refinery, that would go all the way down to Domino Sugar, that was the refinery bus. Then you had the one that would stop at Delery Street. So there were only two buses. Now bear in mind those were the only two buses that were coming down in the Lower Ninth Ward, but that was on the outskirts of the Lower Ninth Ward. So if you were in the inner part, like where

I was living, that's like about 10 blocks. You had to walk 10 blocks to catch the bus. If you were on Law Street or one of those streets, which is like maybe about 15 blocks, all those little streets in that Lower Ninth Ward, that's the only bus that's coming down there, and that bus only runs till about 11 o'clock, I think it was, 11 or 12 o'clock. So if you missed the bus coming down there, you've got to walk, and it didn't have no street lights and whatnot. It was dark down there. You know, like the country.

Ken McCarthy: The Lower Ninth is a big area.

Roger Lewis: Yeah, that's what I'm trying to tell you. Later on, they started running the Galvez bus down through there, then the Barracks bus. That came way later in the game.

The Ninth Ward had its own thing, as far as music. You had the Lasties. You had George Davis, you had Eddie Bo, of course, you had Fats Domino, Ernest McLean...They had a lot of clubs that you could play in the Lower Ninth Ward. They had what we called joints, ballrooms, you know where cats be playing their jam sessions.

They had a club called Freddie Domino. Man, it would be dark back up there, around Law Street. There are no lights, and cats would roll up and come to a little joint like in the woods, off the forbidden path, where they'd be having jam sessions, serious jam sessions. See, there were so many places where people were playing jazz and blues.

It was like you were saying, you go to Bourbon Street, and you think that's it, but when you start venturing out into the city - different parts of the city where they tell you, "Don't go" - that's where all the good music at. Back in the day, we used to play in a club called Darrow's. That's in the Seventh Ward where the Indians used to hold their Indian practice. And that was even before a club called the Glass House, which was famous. The Glass House became a very famous club. It was like somebody's garage, their storage room, and they turned it into a club. You could put about 25 people in there. In fact, we put about 50 or 75 in there in that place [Laughing]. And it was in a neighborhood you ain't supposed to be going, people are getting robbed and everything else is happening to them, but people were steady coming.

Ken McCarthy: That was in the Seventh Ward?

Roger Lewis: No, that was Uptown. Darrow's was in the Seventh Ward. That's the first club, we used to play at on the weekend. The Glass House, we played during the week. The Glass House became really famous because a lot of musicians used to come through there. One night I remember Fats Domino was sitting at the bar. Bernard Purdie and Dizzy Gillespie were sitting at the table in the front, and Manhattan Transfer was in the back of the room.

Ken McCarthy: Wow.

Roger Lewis: When musicians used to come to New Orleans they would always come to the Glass House. That's where the Dirty Dozen was playing. We used to be rockin' that place. Then the music created a dance style called buck jumping, that real fancy footwork that kids be doing now.

Ken McCarthy: So that's where that started? It started with the Dirty Dozen Brass Band music?

Roger Lewis: Yeah, that particular style. What's happening now with brass bands is that they're not really - I mean they're still playing with that New Orleans feeling and the young kids are doing what they're doing, but they're not really playing a lot of traditional New Orleans music. I think there's only one brass band around that I've heard that's really carrying on the real tradition, other than the Preservation Hall Jazz Band, and that's the Hot 8 Brass Band. I just did a CD with those guys. That's carrying on the tradition of pretty much what we were doing, but not none of those bands play the music of Bird, Charlie Parker like what we were doing. That takes a lot of set down. And some of them don't want to set down and pay them kind of dues, man. They were playin' "Dexterity" and "Chippin'" and we used to play "Sidewinder" and "Night in Tunisia." Matter of fact, we did a show with Dizzy Gillespie. Actually, Dizzy Gillespie recorded with us on, I think it was *Voodoo*; him and Branford Marsalis. And we did a thing at the Orpheum Theatre back in the '80s. And I didn't know they had a recording of that. They're getting ready to put it out, too.

Ken McCarthy: Oh, really?

Roger Lewis: Dizzy sitting in with the Dirty Dozen. There are about four or five songs he played on. It's beautiful.

Ken McCarthy: What's the label?

Roger Lewis: There's a group out of New Orleans called Galactic, they're getting ready to put it out. But getting back to the Ninth Ward, the Ninth Ward had its own thing. Uptown had its own thing.

Ken McCarthy: Can I interrupt you just a second on that? How old were you, roughly, when your family moved to the Ninth Ward?

Roger Lewis: Let's see. I started playing music at eight years old when I was living uptown. That was 1948. Got a saxophone in 1950? I guess I was about 15 or 16 maybe.

Ken McCarthy: Okay, so a lot of your musical development took place in the Irish Channel or Uptown or in Garden District?

Roger Lewis: Yeah. I started playing piano. Piano was my first instrument. Then I got a saxophone when we were living in Irish Channel actually in 1950. Then we moved - I played in the high school band so that's probably around '57. I'd say around '58 is when we moved down to the Lower Ninth Ward.

Ken McCarthy: And what kind of music were you hearing as a kid? Obviously the church music. Were you hearing club music at night? Maybe coming through the window?

Roger Lewis: Well, you know, we didn't have television. So you had radio. You'd stick your ear to the radio. As a kid, I was into a lot of country and western music.

Ken McCarthy: Really?

Roger Lewis: Yeah. You know, *"Oh, give me a home where the buffalo roam and the deer and the antelope play. Where seldom is heard, a discouraging word and the sky is not cloudy all day. Home, home on the range, where the deer and the antelope play. Where seldom is heard, a discouraging word and the sky is not cloudy all day."* Oh, yeah, man, I love that song.

Ken McCarthy: People don't realize how much country western music flowed around. It got everywhere.

Roger Lewis: Then you had zydeco music and all that stuff was happening too.

Ken McCarthy: Really, that was already happening when you were a boy?

Roger Lewis: Oh yeah. Man, a lot of people don't know about that part of the history down in Lafayette and all that.

Ken McCarthy: Did you hear that on the radio?

Roger Lewis: Not so much of that. You'd just hear that coming up. Then a lot of classical music. Matter of fact, I used to listen to a lot of classical music coming up, because that would be an opera. A lot of that music would be on the radio.

Ken McCarthy: There are stories about Louis Armstrong going to the opera house and standing outside as a little boy just to listen.

Roger Lewis: Oh, yeah. That was a part of my culture coming up because we had that kind of stuff in the school system.

[End of excerpt.]

Listen to the full interview at:
www.JazzOnTheTube.com/NOLA

Ornette Remembers New Orleans

Ornette was 77 at the time of recording. The time he's referring to is 1949, when he was 19 years old. Recorded February 27, 2007

Ornette Coleman: I used to live with Melvin Lastie's family. Did you ever hear of Melvin Lastie?

Ken McCarthy: He was a trumpet player?

Ornette Coleman: A trumpet player from New Orleans. He had two or three brothers. I stayed with them. I don't remember telling you this story, but their mother and they were kind of like spiritual, religious. One morning I had gotten up early and she was sitting on the porch and said, "Ornette, come here. Go there and bring me that money." She said "Just keep walking. I'll tell you when to stop." And I did. Stopped. Bent down, and there was money.

Ken McCarthy: Just in the street?

Ornette Coleman: Well, it was kinda like, lots of plants. You know when you're going in a back alley. It was a community. And it was full of... grass was growing, and leaves and trees. And it was like, say, if you were going into the backyard of somebody's place. Well, it was kind of like that. Melvin Lastie's mother asked me to walk there, and stop, and she said, "Ok, it's there." And when I bent down, the money was there and I got it and brought it to her.

Ken McCarthy: Wow.

Ornette Coleman: It was nothing that was planned. Just, "Ornette, come here. Do this, do that." And I'd done exactly what she asked me to do. And it was what she said.

Ken McCarthy: Somehow she knew there was money there?

Ornette Coleman: Yeah. She didn't say "I lost some money."

Ken McCarthy: I'll show you this book I got when I was down there. (*Spirit World* by Michael Smith.) It reminded me of some of the things that you were telling me about that you experienced when you were in New Orleans.

Ornette Coleman: Oh, that's good. ... Melvin Lastie would play the trumpet. I stayed with his family. I found myself in New Orleans by myself and I met Melvin and I was staying at his house. It was really beautiful. I mean, when I say beautiful, it was very human. And very good.

Ken McCarthy: It still is that way. That's what I am so attracted to about it, and why I keep going back.

Ornette Coleman: Yeah. I wasn't playing too much there. I mean, I was playing, but I wasn't making any money.

Ken McCarthy: You once told me a story about playing in the church.

Ornette Coleman: Yeah. I'd go to church and play just the way I'm playing when I play a job.

Ken McCarthy: And everybody accepted it and understood it.

Ornette Coleman: Yeah. And, you know, I was really free then, believe me. I was playing real free. Which I'm still doing. I mean, what I call free. I don't design something and then play that, you know? Not only that I went to church a lot, which was really different, too. New Orleans is a real spiritual place. And the people are really, really good. And the food is good.

Ken McCarthy: The food is incredible.

Ornette Coleman: The food is good.

Ken McCarthy: I'd go there just to eat.

Ornette Coleman: The food is good. It was very American as far as I'm concerned. It reminded me of where I was born, Fort Worth, and a little kid. The people were very kind and very creative, and very spiritual. I used to go to church in New Orleans, you know, the spiritual church. And the people would get up and testify. And tears coming out. It was real, that's all I can say. I can't say I had a happy time because it was more than happiness, it was like your soul being - what is the right word - being allowed to be shown.

I think I got to New Orleans when I was with Pee Wee Creighton, a southern blues and rhythm guy that went there, and I went on the road with him and ended up in New Orleans. And I met Melvin Lastie. Have you heard him play?

Ken McCarthy: I don't think I ever have, no.

Ornette Coleman: The way he was playing, I mean - the way Clifford Brown, Miles Davis, and those guys were playing jazz, I mean playing their ideas, he was playing much more stronger rhythms. It was really beautiful. I don't know if he's still living. He kind of stutters a little. And his father was a preacher.

Ken McCarthy: Has he ever been recorded, do you think?

Ornette Coleman: I heard that he has, but I have never found a record that anyone has given to me.

Ken McCarthy: I'll look for one. That sounds very interesting.

Ornette Coleman: Yeah.

Ken McCarthy: They have a great sense of feeling for rhythms down there that's unique.

Ornette Coleman: Yeah.

Ken McCarthy: Like when I would hear Ed Blackwell play.

Ornette Coleman: Yeah.

Ken McCarthy: I didn't know anything about New Orleans. But when I first heard him play I was amazed.

Ornette Coleman: Yeah, that's true. Blackwell was from there. New Orleans is a very unique place for all races, for the human race, basically.

Ken McCarthy: There seems to be a lot of kindness amongst people down there. And everybody encourages each other's creativity. And I'm sad to say you don't see that much in America, in other parts of America. It seems to be losing that.

Ornette Coleman: That's right. And especially, the races themselves don't seem to be affected because of what classification the races are. It seems that the quality of how they exist makes it much happier for everybody. And that's what I experienced. And the music is free soul. It's totally free soul. Beautiful. I haven't been there in a long time, since I've grown up and started making records and stuff. But I'd like to go there and play one day. I'd like to take my band and play.

Ken McCarthy: Yeah.

Ornette Coleman: I'd like to get me a booking there to play... I mean, maybe I would go there just to visit, take my horn, and...

Ken McCarthy: I have to say every time I go down, I have the best time of my life.

Ornette Coleman: I believe it.

Ken McCarthy: The food, the people, the musical culture.

Ornette Coleman: I can imagine that. I know that's true.

[End of transcript.]

Listen to the audio recording of this conversation, and the complete 'Remembering Ornette' Collection at:

www.JazzOnTheTube.com/NOLA

(1) Jazz on the Tube: Ken and Ornette Talk About New Orleans

(2) Jazz on the Tube: Complete 'Remembering Ornette' Collection

See Appendix for more details.

THE KATRINA MYTH: THE TRUTH ABOUT A THOROUGHLY UNNATURAL DISASTER

Film produced and script
by Ken McCarthy for Levees.org
Released in the summer of 2008

Starting on August 29th, 2005, the biggest catastrophe to ever befall an American city in peacetime took place in New Orleans. Over 800,000 people were driven from their homes. At least 1,482 were killed, and 80% of the city's buildings and infrastructure lay underwater for weeks. Estimates of the total economic damage to the city are at least $100 billion dollars. In spite of the enormity of the disaster and the extensive media coverage it received, few people understand what really happened in New Orleans, or what caused it. Fewer still realize that they too may be living under a similar or even greater threat. In this video, we expose the key myths and misunderstandings about the New Orleans flood and the role the U.S. Army Corps of Engineers played in the city's near-destruction.

Myth #1: Katrina was a "natural disaster"

The number one myth about what happened in New Orleans is that it was a natural disaster. This is false. Though the storm did do some wind damage to the city, this damage could have been repaired within a few months, if not weeks. What catastrophically damaged 80% of the city was flooding. And the flooding was caused by a major systemic failure by the federally funded U.S. Army Corps of Engineers levee system.

The levees and floodwalls, designed and built at the cost of millions of U.S. taxpayer dollars, failed in 53 different places. In two neighborhoods, Lakeview and the Lower Ninth Ward, the levee walls totally collapsed, sending walls of water crashing into houses and businesses at velocities capable of moving structures off of their foundations and tossing cars like toys. Other neighborhoods sat in salty or brackish, contaminated floodwater for a month or more because dozens of pumps were rendered useless due to canal wall failures along the discharge channels.

Ray Seed, a professor of civil engineering at the University of California at Berkeley, who participated in an in-depth study of the New Orleans flooding, called it the most expensive engineering failure in American history, and quite possibly the second most expensive in human history, second only to the Chernobyl nuclear power plant failure. The catastrophic flooding of New Orleans was a man-made engineering disaster, not a natural one.

Myth #2: Located so close to the Gulf of Mexico, New Orleans is in the wrong place

During the levee failure catastrophe, while thousands remained stranded in the city without food, water, or medical care, some claimed that the source of New Orleans' troubles was that it was located in the wrong place. Again, this is false.

Situated at the end of the Mississippi River, New Orleans is the literal gateway to America's agricultural and industrial heartland. Upstream of New Orleans, the Mississippi River becomes too shallow to allow for the passing of ocean-going freighters and container ships. Therefore New Orleans and the land it sits on has historically been, is now, and in all likelihood will probably always be one of the most important ports and shipping points in the United States.

New Orleans used to be much better protected against the impact of hurricanes and other storms. When it was founded the city was located 125 miles from the Gulf of Mexico and sheltered by hundreds of square miles of wetland which acted as a buffer against storms and storm surges. The reckless dredging of over 10,000 miles of canals by the U.S. Army Corps of Engineers, as well as damages caused by oil and shipping interests, has fractured and undermined this protective barrier. To date, almost none of this damage has been repaired, and what is left of the natural marsh continues to erode.

Myth #3: New Orleans is below sea level, and its residents are putting themselves in harm's way by living there

The Lower Ninth Ward, which was devastated by the flood, is actually above sea level. So, too, are the city's originally settled areas, including the French Quarter, the central business district, the Garden District, Treme, the Marigny, Bywater, and Uptown. While it is true that parts of New Orleans are below sea level, New Orleans is not the only major coastal city that faces flooding challenges.

In New York City, for instance, much of the city's transportation system, including its subways and tunnels, lie below sea level and require 24-hour-a-day pumping to remain dry. London, the biggest city in Europe and one of the most important financial centers in the world, depends on a massive flood barrier to stay above water during storms.

And then there's Holland. For over 400 years, this prosperous and technologically advanced nation has had 24% of its land mass, including its most populated cities and towns, below sea level. The country survives because of a well-conceived, well-built, and well-maintained levee system.

Interestingly, cities do not have to exist below sea level to flood. Those built above sea level can suffer the same fate. In fact, Fernley, Nevada, located 4200 feet above sea level, flooded when its protective levee collapsed. It is, therefore, not the location of cities that imperils them by flooding, it is improperly built levees that cause disasters. This is what caused the devastation in New Orleans and not the fact that a portion of it is built below sea level.

Myth #4: The situation in New Orleans can't happen elsewhere because the conditions are unique to New Orleans

There are numerous taxpayer-funded U.S. Army Corps of Engineers projects in all 50 states. As much as 43% of all Americans live in a county that has areas protected by one or more levees. Sadly, it is reported that 28 states have levees declared by the Corps itself as being in a state of active failure. Here's a short list of American cities that are so affected: Detroit, Louisville, Nashville, Pittsburgh, Memphis, Baltimore, Kansas City, Omaha, Portland, Seattle, Honolulu, Jacksonville, Savannah, Albuquerque, Los Angeles, Sacramento, and even Washington DC. Many of these places have levees in worse condition than the system New Orleans had in place before it failed.

Surprisingly, the place most at risk for levee failures is Sacramento and the Sacramento River Delta.

Levee failures here would not only devastate Sacramento and Stockton, it would also cause seawater contamination of the only fresh water source now used by more than 23 million Californians. And even worse, such contamination would render the water supply unusable for years.

Myth #5: The authorities are aware of the problem and they are working hard to solve it

The U.S. Army Corps of Engineers has no current plans to change its business-as-usual approach to levee building and maintenance. With a few rare exceptions, no politicians appear to be interested in examining, let alone addressing, this situation at all. Currently, the U.S. Army Corps of Engineers has no governmental agency or department to oversee their projects with any meaningful authority. Consequently, it's just a matter of time before the kind of catastrophe that struck New Orleans is repeated in other parts of the country. If this situation is going to change for the better, it will rest in the hands and on the shoulders of individual citizens pressuring Congress, the White House, state governors, and local officials.

To learn what you can do to turn this situation around and make sure New Orleans and the rest of the country doesn't suffer the same fate as New Orleans did in 2005, visit Levees.org.

This is a grassroots, non-partisan group of dedicated individuals who work to educate citizens about the ongoing levee failure risks to New Orleans, southern Louisiana, and the rest of the nation.

With your help, we can save lives as well as entire communities and cultures.

Please visit Levees.org.

***

Watch "The Katrina Myth" video at: www.JazzOnTheTube.com/NOLA

Ken first approached us volunteering his help in January 2007. That day marked a new chapter in our organization's history.

In less than an hour, Ken laid out a strategy for using the Internet and video that we've followed ever since with great success.

Thanks to his ideas we've attracted celebrity spokespersons like John Goodman and Harry Shearer, gotten free television air time for our message, and generated over 225,000 views of our videos on the Internet.

Ken has not only offered advice, he's also rolled up his sleeves and helped and has not stopped helping since that day.

He's brought in experts to help us with every aspect of our media campaign, helped us shape our communication strategy, and wrote and produced "The Katrina Myth" video which has proven to be one of our most effective educational tools.

New Orleans has never had a better friend or more loyal supporter.

Sandy Rosenthal
Founder and Executive Director of Levees.org
Author of "Words Whispered in Water"

WORDS WHISPERED IN WATER

"Sandy Rosenthal is a courageous and indefatigable warrior for justice."
—Dave Eggers

Why the Levees Broke in Hurricane Katrina

SANDY ROSENTHAL
Founder of Levees.org

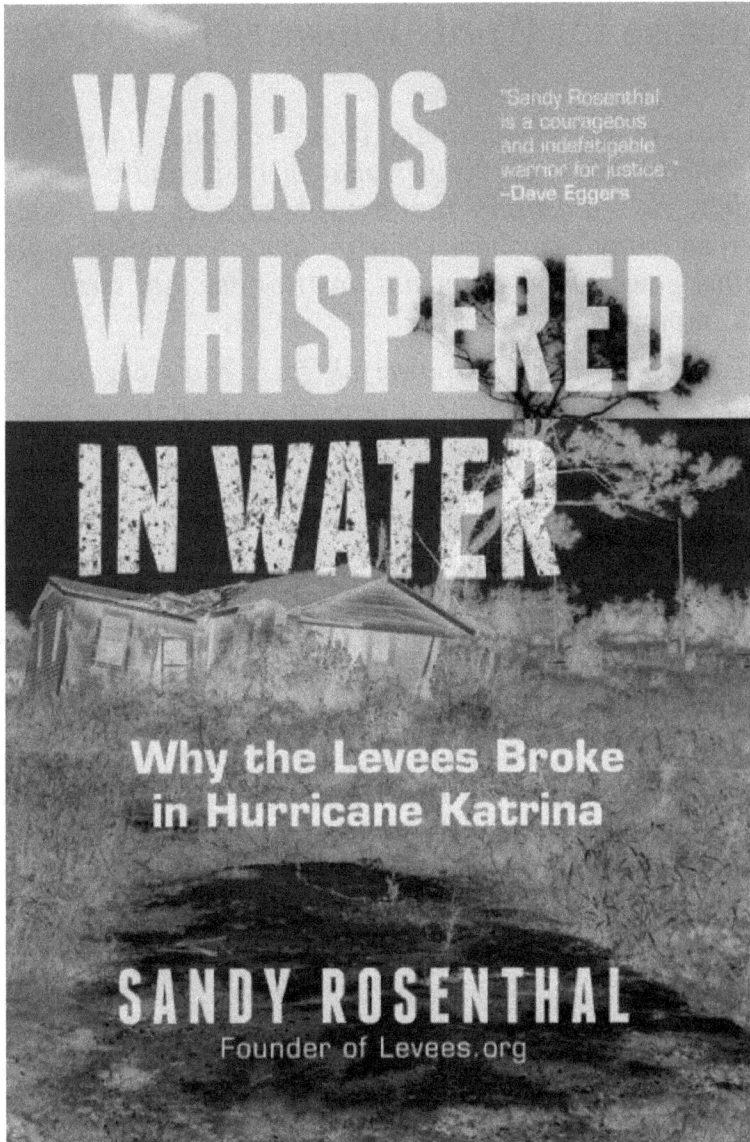

Rosenthal, Sandy. *Words Whispered in Water*. Mango, 2020.

Praise for *Words Whispered in Water*

"This is an extraordinary book – at once an elegantly written thriller, a deeply personal memoir, and a practical guide to citizen action – that appears at the precise moment when so many of us have come to doubt our ability to fight against powerful governmental institutions that seem to act with impunity.

I had heard that a powerful grass roots organization had been organized in the aftermath of the Katrina tragedy to fight the attempt by the US Army Corps of Engineers to hide known design flaws in the flood walls and – using an all too typical bureaucratic trick -- define the rupture of the levees as a "natural" disaster. Defining something as natural, of course, is a sly way of hinting that it is inevitable and caused by forces beyond anyone's ability to prevent. Of course, powerful institutions do whatever they can to make sure those "forces" continue to be seen as natural.

Sandy Rosenthal's vivid account of how she and other activists organized to uncover these design flaws - fatal flaws by people and anything but natural - reveals just how far a powerful institution will go to hide its own failures and just how much relentless tenacity is required for citizens to discover the truth...

The simple lesson of the book, that seemingly unmovable power is often only waiting for someone with the courage and persistence to move it, is probably more important today than at any time I can remember."

- From a review by Steven M. Gorelick

EPILOGUE: MELODY MAKERS ("LIL' LIZA JANE")

by Chuck Perkins

This is for my artists of virtuosity
Who kept the music in the mystery.
For my artistic vanguard
Who came back when times were hard.
Who sometimes came back to nothing
But still came back, underrated and uninsured
Putting their horn where their mouth is.

This is for my buckjumping pied pipers,
Second lining my people back home.

This is for my melody makers,
For my cowbell ringers
And my tambourine shakers.

It's for the Lady Buckjumpers,
the Rebirth Brass Band,
And The Storyville Stompers.

It's for the Soul Rebels
And the Hot Eight,
For the Lil Rascals wanting a dime
When all they got is eight.

It's for Kermit Ruffins
And The Barbecue Swingers,
For Marva Wright,
And all my blues singers.

For making that music
That heal our pain.
It's for Shannon Powell,
And Lil Liza Jane.

I got Liza
You got Liza
We got Liza

I'm from the NOLA,
And I thought I told ya.
It's for the Golden Comanche,
And the Wild Magnolias.

We love her scat
And we love your razzle dazzle,
It's for Irvin Mayfield
And Germaine Bazzle.

It's for loving our city
We ain't given up an inch,
It's for Stanton Moore,
Bob and George French.

It's for Dr Michael White
For keeping it tight,
And for Uncle Lionel
Still raising hell.

We sho gon miss him when we die.

It's for Troy Sawyer,
And Kevin O'Day,
"Kid Chocolate" Brown,
And John Boutté.

It's for Dave Torkanowsky
And Walter Wolfman,

For Trombone Shorty,
And the whole Andrews clan,
And the Marsalis clan,
And the Batiste clan, too,
Charmaine Neville,
This poem's for you,
And don't forget Kidd Jordan
And the whole Jordan crew.

It's for Phillip Manuel
And Leah Chase,
Herlin Riley on drums,
Roland Guerin on bass.

Holla' if you hear me.
It's for Corey Henry on trombone,
Kirk Joseph on sousaphone,
Donald Harrison on sax.
I take off my hat for Benny Jones
And Leroy Jones and all our musicians
Who came back home.

This poem's for you.

We'll work today
If you play tonight.
Sing us a song
That makes us all right.
The sounds of your horns
Give us strength to fight.

We'll gut the houses
If you play your sax
And we'll swing the hammer
If you swing your ax.
We'll work with haste
Just you play your drum
Please bring the bass
And we'll have some fun
Run with the sounds
As hot as the sun
Buma bum bum bum bum
Play ya drum.
Son, put down your gun
Let's have some fun.
Work during the day
But when the night time come.

Watch Chuck Perkins perform this poem live in New Orleans at:
www.JazzOnTheTube.com/NOLA

(1) Lil' Liza Jane - Live at Chickie Wah Wah. Produced and directed by Ken McCarthy.

See Appendix for more details.

VOICES OF THE BIG EASY

CHUCK PERKINS

A LOVE SONG FOR NOLA

12 MUSIC POEMS

Perkins, Chuck. *Voices of the Big Easy, A Love Song For NOLA.*
2012

Praise for *A Love Song For NOLA*

"CD Of The Year? This homage to New Orleans and tribute to the people of that city before during and after Katrina struck is a true passionate love story laced with rage against the Blanco's and Bushe's of the federal and local governments. Perkin's words are pure passionate poetry that at times flow like the torrents of water that cascaded through the streets of New Qrleans. Pure poetry. The voice and the music complement each other. Listen to the first track Jazz Funeral, and you'll be hooked. Jazz, African, creole, Indian, such a brilliant mix of music. This is a powerful, angry, and beautiful CD. Can there be a better one this year? I can't see it. Buy this CD it's brilliant"

- From a review by Mickey Dipp

APPENDIX I: VIDEOS & OTHER RESOURCES

Dive deeper into the music of New Orleans at:
www.JazzontheTube.com/NOLA

Many of the people, events, and conversations mentioned in this book are on video or audio that can be found on the JazzontheTube.com site.

Videos / Audios

John Swenson

(1) *The Making of Glen David Andrews' "Walking Through Heaven's Gate."* Directed and edited by Lily Keber. Funded by Ken McCarthy.

(2) *Helen Hill Funeral.* Filmed by Ken McCarthy.

(3) *Dinerral Shavers in the 2006 Big Nine parade.* Filmed by Julie Carruth. (2006)

(4) *Glen David Andrews at the "Silence Is Violence rally" at City Hall, New Orleans.* (2007)

Bonus Videos:

(5) *Smokey Johnson and Bob French talk about New Orleans drummers. At the Ponderosa Stomp.* (2008)

(6) *Farewell Spotted Cat - The Shout.* Filmed by Ken McCarthy.

(7) *Defending the Mardi Gras Indians.* Produced by Ken McCarthy.

(8) *Eddie Bo at the Sound Café.* (2008) Filmed by Ken McCarthy.

(9) *Aurora Nealand at the Spotted Cat.* (Fall 2006) Filmed by Ken McCarthy.

Glen David Andrews

(1) *Glen David Andrews at the "Silence Is Violence rally" at City Hall, New Orleans.* (2007)

(2) *Glen David Andrews, "Easter Sunday Parking Lot Jam."* (2009) Filmed by Ken McCarthy.

Ronald Lewis

Chuck Perkins interviews Ronald Lewis. Directed and edited by Hugie Vigreux. Produced by Ken McCarthy.

Roger Lewis

Jazz on the Tube: *Roger Lewis and the Good News from New Orleans*

Ornette Coleman

(1) Jazz on the Tube: *Ken and Ornette Talk About New Orleans*

(2) Jazz on the Tube: Complete 'Remembering Ornette' Collection

(3) Podcast: Marble, Matt. *The Black Hawk Chant - Mothers Leafy Anderson and Catherine Seals.* Secret Sound.

(4) Podcast: *Mother Catherine Seals And The Temple Of The Innocent Blood.* TriPod: New Orleans at 300

(5) Podcast: *The Legendary Lasties.* TriPod: New Orleans at 300

(6) Podcast: *TriPod Xtras: Herlin Riley And Joe Lastie.* TriPod: New Orleans at 300

Levees.org

The Katrina Myth. Written and produced by Ken McCarthy. Directed and edited by Chrispin Barnes.

Chuck Perkins

(1) *Lil' Liza Jane - Live at Chickie Wah Wah.* Produced and directed by Ken McCarthy.

(2) *We Ain't Dead Yet.* Produced & Directed by Ken McCarthy.

(3) *Congo Square.* Produced & Directed by Ken McCarthy.

(4) *Chuck Perkins in Liverpool and Manchester.* A film by Ken McCarthy.

(5) *English Poet Grevel Lindop in New Orleans.* A film by Ken McCarthy.

Recommended Reading, Listening, and Viewing

Music & Poetry

(1) Perkins, Chuck. *A Lovesong For NOLA*. Trikont, 2012

Documentaries

(1) *Tradition Is a Temple*. A film by Darren Hoffman. *(2013)*

Collectively, Jazz on the Tube subscribers were major financial supporters of this excellent documentary that gets to the heart of why New Orleans has such a rich musical culture. Among other things, they invest in their children.

(2) *The City of a Million Dreams*. A film by Jason Berry. (2019)

Books

(1) Swenson, John. *New Atlantis: Musicians Battle for the Survival of New Orleans*. Oxford University Press, 2011

(2) Lewis, Ronald. *The House of Dance & Feathers*. UNO Press/Neighborhood Story Project, 2009

(3) Sullivan, Jack. *New Orleans Remix*. University Press of Mississippi. 2017

(4) Smith, Michael. *Spirit World: Pattern in the Expressive Folk Culture of New Orleans*. Pelican Publishing Company, 1992

(5) Rosenthal, Sandy. *Words Whispered in Water*. Mango, 2020

(6) Berry, J., Foose, J., Jones, T. *Up from the Cradle of Jazz: New Orleans Music Since World War II*. University of Georgia Press, 1986

(7) Berry, Jason. *The Spirit of Black Hawk: A Mystery of Africans and Indians.* University Press of Mississippi, 1995

(8) Berry, Jason. *City of a Million Dreams: A History of New Orleans at Year 300.* The University of North Carolina Press, 2018

(9) Kennedy, Al. *Chord Changes on the Chalkboard: How Public School Teachers Shaped Jazz and the Music of New Orleans.* Scarecrow Press, 2005

Websites

(1) JazzontheTube.com - Thousands of jazz videos with extensive New Orleans material.

(2) ACloserWalkNOLA.com - New Orleans music history, block by block.

(3) OffBeat.com - The daily guide to all things musical in New Orleans and Louisiana.

Museums

(1) Treme's Petit Jazz Museum - Al Jackson, proprietor

https://www.facebook.com/tremespetitjazzmuseum

1500 Governor Nicholls St, New Orleans, LA 70116

1 504-715-0332

(2) Backstreet Cultural Museum

https://www.backstreetmuseum.org

1531 St Philip St, New Orleans, LA 70116

1 504-657-6700

Appendix II:
Quickstart Guide to
New Orleans

Dive deeper into
the music of New Orleans at:
www.JazzontheTube.com/NOLA

Going Deep in the Big Easy

New Orleans is deep (probably the deepest city in the U.S. — and by far measure), but it doesn't give up its depth easily.

It took me many months living there just to get my bearings, and what I realized when I did was that the place is so deep there is probably no ever getting to the bottom of it.

You can certainly see some beautiful sights, eat some great food, and stumble on some great music without much or even any preparation, but if you want to start touching the depth sooner rather than later, a little preparation will take you a long way.

First, check the calendar and weather. Unless you are used to SERIOUS tropical heat — May to October is intense. It's not the heat. It's the humidity.

Second, on your first visit, I recommend you avoid big events like Mardi Gras, Jazz Fest, spring break, and holidays (the one exception being St. Patrick's/ St. Joseph's Day.) On "off" times, it's a calmer, more leisurely place, easier to navigate, and with better deals on hotels. Once you've broken the ice and learned the ropes, by all means, come back for one of the festive times and enjoy those, too.

Seven Simple Steps to Get to Know New Orleans Fast

Step One: Tune into WWOZ.org which, thanks to the Internet, you can do from anywhere in the world. Here you'll discover that this one relatively small city produces so much music that it needs an entire 24/7/365 radio station to represent just a fraction of it.

Step Two: Visit OffBeat.com. You'll probably encounter some music and names on WWOZ you've never heard before. Offbeat Magazine is the Encyclopedia Britannica of New Orleans and Louisiana music and there's so much music there, the city really needs one. Also like WWOZ, Offbeat produces a daily music calendar — much needed because a "slow" music day in New Orleans would be the height of many other city's music seasons.

Step Three: Study up on the food in advance. There is no reason to ever have a bad meal in New Orleans and you could literally spend a year (or years) eating great things here before you ever repeat yourself, but as a first-time visitor, you may fall prey to the tourist traps which exist everywhere. OffBeat.com has great food reviews and is a good place to start. A little Internet research here will make a world of difference in your experience.

Step Four: ACloserWalkNOLA.com. This is the best online cultural-geographic New Orleans resource I know of. Take advantage of it.

Step Five: CitySightSeeingNewOrleans.com. Once you're settled in and are ready to see the city, get on the Hop-On Hop-Off bus. New Orleans has a lot of moving parts and it's very helpful to get an overview first. Some of the city's best must-see neighborhoods like the French Quarter and the Garden District are far apart and this service will let you see both. It stops in many places in the city.

Step Six: Treme's Petit Jazz Museum. This tiny museum in the heart of The Treme, a neighborhood every visitor should visit, is the best place to get started on the long and pleasant journey of getting to know New Orleans. Al Jackson is your guide and I can't think of a better way to start to get to know the depth of the city's cultural history than to visit with him.

Step Seven: Frenchmen Street. Great music can be found in literally every corner of the city, but if you want a lot of great music in one concentrated place, these three blocks are the places to get started.

ABOUT THE AUTHOR

Ken McCarthy was one of the early pioneers of the movement to commercialize the Internet in the early 1990s. *Time* Magazine credits him with being the first person to recognize and articulate the importance of the click-through rate as a key metric for making the Internet commercially viable.

He was also a pioneer of, and in some cases directly initiated, the use of many now-common Internet publishing activities: email marketing (1994), banner advertising (1994), A/B split testing (1996), e-mail auto-responders (1996), blogging (1997), push-button audio content (now known as "podcasting") (2002), online video (2005), and mobile marketing (2008).

At various times, he's been involved in the business side of music as a radio show host, a concert producer, and a grunt at a New York City record label. In 2008, he started a website devoted to jazz videos which has evolved into one of the most visited jazz websites on the Internet, JazzontheTube.com.

About the Publisher

The publisher of this book, JazzontheTube.com, is the biggest annotated and indexed online collection of jazz videos on earth – and it's free.

We deliver great jazz videos to our fans all over the world every day.

Jazz on the Tube provides five services:

1. A searchable archive of thousands of carefully hand-picked and annotated jazz videos

2. A free Video-of-the-Day service. Love jazz? We deliver a great jazz video to your mailbox every day. You can subscribe for free.

3. The Internet's only free up-to-date worldwide directory of jazz clubs, festivals, radio stations, educational programs, and organizations.

4. The Jazz on the Tube podcast series which features in-depth interviews on the history – and future – of the music with a focus on scholars, educators, and presenters.

5. A detailed educational resource on the music of Cuba and other Latin countries, and their underreported, and often under-appreciated, impact on jazz past, present, and future.

Why do we do this?

We do this because we love the music, the people who make it, and the people who listen to it!

If you'd like to support our efforts, please become a subscriber (it's free), watch some great videos, and then go out and hear some great LIVE music.

Free subscriptions are available here:

JazzontheTube.com

www.ingramcontent.com/pod-product-compliance
Lightning Source LLC
Chambersburg PA
CBHW070835100426

42813CB00003B/621